CULTURE CHANGE IN AN INTERTRIBAL MARKET

CULTURE CHANGE IN AN INTERTRIBAL MARKET

THE ROLE OF THE BANARI INTERTRIBAL MARKET AMONG THE HILL PEOPLES OF CHOTANAGPUR

D. P. SINHA

ASIA PUBLISHING HOUSE
LONDON

Dharnidhar Prasad Sinha (1934)

PRINTED IN INDIA
BY BHOLANATH HAZRA AT RUPABANI PRESS, 31, BIPLABI PULIN DAS STREET, CALCUTTA-9 AND PUBLISHED BY P. S. JAYASINGHE, ASIA PUBLISHING HOUSE, 447 STRAND, LONDON W.C. 2

To

MY PARENTS

whose patience, faith and encouragement
has been a constant source of inspiration

FOREWORD

On the fringes of industrialization all over the world the industrial system is penetrating the economies of tribal and peasant peoples. Westerners, viewing the process from outside, call it "development". Most of us think of such "development" as inevitable. Many regard it as "good". It represents the kind of "progress" to which we are heavily committed.

To an anthropologist, however, such a value judgment is premature, even presumptious. He may ask : Does economic development engender a one-way process toward industrialization on the part of a non-industrialized community, as is often assumed ? Is the common stereotype of a progressively higher "standard of living" being engendered in such a community through the contact situation substantiated by the facts ?

There is only one way to arrive at an acceptable answer to these questions. "Development", like any other cultural phenomenon, must be investigated. It must be examined as a process. It must be analysed as a complex event in situational and historical context without prejudice and without prior commitment.

Hence there arises the questions how can we isolate the process of "development" ? How can such a complex contact situation be brought under the microscope so to speak ? How can it be investigated systematically by the methods of science ?

Karl Polanyi made us aware of the modern self-regulating market as the focal institution of the "free" enterprise system. In delineating the nature of the "free" market, his researches in economic history and comparative economics illuminated the entire industrial system. For the first time we were able fully to appreciate the modern self-regulating market as a unique cultural phenomenon of international scope, in sharp contrast to the many locally self-contained markets found throughout history in the non-industrialised world. We could then pinpoint a relevant question. What happens when the "free" enterprise market encroaches on a locally self-contained market ?

Many studies have been made of tribal markets either separately or as part of more comprehensive general ethnographic descriptions of the culture of a social group. We needed a study focusing on the many-sided contact situation itself as a process operating between different kinds of social groups at many different levels. We needed to pursue the ramifications of the process wherever they might lead.

Now D. P. Sinha has described one such local market on the basis of detailed first-hand observations recorded over an extended period of time. He has portrayed the role of the Banari intertribal market of Chotanagpur in its regional setting, its social matrix, and in historical, even pre-historical, perspective. He has traced with great care the sequence of occasions and events by which the Banari market and its constituents are being drawn into, and related to, the international market system.

The analysis skilfully illuminates many areas of current interest in anthropology. But its most important contribution perhaps stems from its treatment of the phenomena of culture change as multilevel multiway process which may be investigated by means of presently available precise field methods.

The search for heuristic approaches and precise methodology for the scientific study of cultural phenomena has led to many new developments in anthropology. We note, particularly, recent advances in the microanalysis of languages, social structure, artifacts, folklore, cultural values, and patterns of cognitive classification. Achievements in these and other areas of problem have given descriptions of cultural phenomena a new precision. It is hoped that these may serve as the factual basis for valid classifications of cultural phenomena and for comparative studies from which may emerge a universally valid theory of culture.

In the absence of such a theory it is easy to succumb to reductionism. Since most of the world's cultures are changing at relatively rapid rates we need a deductive theory of culture which focuses on change. We need a comprehensive theory based on the results of the microanalysis of cultural phenomena which will help us to understand the processes of culture change as they actually occur. It must be applicable not only to tribal societies but also to peasant communities and to the urban centers of industrialized nations.

Dr. Sinha's analysis of the Banari market shows us how an intertribal market may afford a significant unit of research for such types of scientific problems. Since the market serves as the contact point between tribal peoples, peasant groups, and agents from the national government and the industrialized world, if viewed in situational context it may be regarded as an ideal natural "laboratory" for observing an experiment in culture change. The main advantage of such a laboratory probably lies in its availability for field work of the meticulous, case counting type in the classic anthropological tradition. I refer to field work involving the observation and accurate recording of the detailed occasions and events of contact and its aftermath over a period of years.

The intertribal market of course has a locus. It is set in a region which may be described in terms of its ecological, climatic, and geological zones. From the viewpoint of natural resources it is traditionally self-sufficient. The market is also the focus of a network of kinship, social, economic, and ceremonial ties and obligations. These cut across ethnic, cultural. linguistic, class, caste, and geographic boundaries. The market is the center of an economic redistributing system involving barter, ceremonial exchange, money and credit. It is the place of gossip, news, games and festivals. It has recently become the regional centre for tax collection, police supervision, mail distribution, propaganda, political activity, public health, education, and community development. Its spatial arrangement reflects both the socio-economic pattern of the region and the process by which urban influences are instigating cultural change in the region. The market is rooted in a long history, many aspects of which underlie present-day behavior patterns of its constituents and play a role in setting future trends.

Here then an anthropologist may observe at first hand and study in depth an ongoing experiment in culture change and "development". What is happening ? What new functions is the market serving ? What new roles are being created ? What innovations are materializing and how do these affect traditional behaviors, attitudes, and values ? How is the intertribal market affecting the impact of culture change in the region ? How are urban and rural lifeways being related ?

These and many more intriguing questions are discussed by Dr. Sinha as he unfolds, step by step in colorful detail, the story of the Banari market in depth. In his case study of the Birhor, he not only traces the activities of one tribal unit in relation to the Banari market, but he also adds another dimension to his previous descriptions of his fascinating tribe of semi-nomadic monkey hunters and their fortunes in the modern world.

On the basis of the facts presented and their inter-relationships, Dr. Sinha then formulates a series of working hypotheses which pinpoint some areas of problem for future investigators. He indicates some of the ways by which agents of change from the outside may tend to disrupt the balance of a traditionally self-sustaining economy. The intertribal market and similar institutions afford a traditional mechanism by which an orderly relationship may be established between tribal and peasant communities on the one hand and agents from modern industrialized centres on the other.

I recommend Dr. Sinha's study not only to all those interested in trying to understand the processes of economic "development" as a whole objectively and form the inside as it were, but also to those seeking a precise multi-dimensional method for the observation and analysis of a total complex situation involving multiway processes of culture change.

Brooklyn

LAURA THOMPSON

PREFACE

THIS BOOK is based upon the research reported in my dissertation presented to the faculty of the Graduate School of Southern Illinois University in spring 1964. The field work was carried out in Banari and its region in Chotanagpur, Bihar, India, during 1957-61, under the auspices of the Department of Anthropology, University of Ranchi. A Fulbright scholarship from the United States Government enabled me to complete the dissertation and a research grant from the Australian National University helped me to revisit the field in 1966 and prepare the manuscript for the present publication. I have, however, restrained myself from revising the text. In the last five years the intertribal market has undergone significant institutional change which, I believe, needs to be reported separately. In passing I may mention that while the market continues to be a vital institution in the region, the Phariyas, its most catalytic agents of change, have almost disappeared from the scene.

The idea for undertaking an institutional analysis of the Banari intertribal market had occurred to me in the mid-'fifties and much of my early thinking on this subject was stimulated by my colleagues and students at the University of Ranchi. Later, in the United States, I had the opportunity of discussing my data with Professor Charles H. Lange and Professor Philip J. C. Dark of Southern Illinois University who took painstaking interest and offered constructive comments while supervising my doctoral dissertation. While I am conscious of the fact that the limitations in this volume are entirely mine, I must express my debt to them for their contributions in making this study possible.

There are two points about this study that I especially wish to mention. First, the use of the term 'intertribal market'. The Banari intertribal market has been traditionally an institution serving tribal peoples of the region. The Hindu castes and the urban traders are relatively new to the scene. While the latter's contribution to the socio-economic components of the Banari intertribal market is rapidly increasing with the growing contacts with the outside world, the market nevertheless retains its intertribal character. I have, therefore, chosen to use the term 'intertribal market' to illustrate a particular 'type' represented by the Banari market. Secondly, my approach in this volume has been, by and large, analytical rather than descriptive. This, I believe, has enabled me in not only reducing the length of this report, but also in presenting my theoretical points as precisely as I could possibly manage.

Many people have contributed to the making of this volume, and to each of them I am equally grateful. I would especially like to express my gratitude to Professor Douglas Oliver of Harvard University, Dr. Alvin W. Wolfe of Washington University at St. Louis, Dr. L. P. Vidyarthi of the University of Ranchi and Mr. B. K. Srivastava of Southern Illinois University for their comments and criticisms during the various phases of research and writing. I am particularly grateful to Professor J. G. Crawford, Director, Research School of Pacific Studies at the Australian National University, for making my revisit to the field possible. The credit for the maps in this volume goes to Mr. Hans Gunther of the Department of Geography, Australian National University. The many ways in which Purnima Chaudhuri Sinha, my wife, helped me to complete this volume can hardly be measured or properly acknowledged.

Finally, I must record my gratitude to Professor Laura Thompson for being generous in contributing a foreward to this publication ; and to Professor Conrad Arensberg for having written an incisive introduction to this small volume.

Canberra D. P. Sinha

CONTENTS

	Foreword by Laura Thompson	*vii*
	Preface	*xi*
	Introduction by Conrad Arensberg	1
I	The Problem	7
II	Approach to the Study of the Banari Intertribal Market	14
III	Ecological Setting of the Banari Intertribal Market	17
IV	Ethnic Components of the Banari Region	29
V	The Banari Intertribal Market	37
VI	Economic Role of the Banari Intertribal Market	59
VII	Social Role of the Banari Intertribal Market	69
VIII	One Tribe in Relation to the Banari Intertribal Market: the Case of the Birhor	81
IX	The Study of the Banari Intertribal Market and its Contributions to Concepts and Theories of Culture Change	92
X	Summary and Conclusion	101
	Glossary	105
	Bibliography	109
	Index	113

PLATES

(Between pages 64 and 65)

I A View of the Market Centre
II Urban Traders Arriving by Bus with Their Trade Goods
III Urban Traders Arriving by Bike
IV Trade Goods Being Transported on Bullock Carts
V A Phariya Arriving with His Horse
VI Oraon Women on Way to The Market
VII A Chik-Baraik Weaver Arriving with His Blankets
VIII Oraon Men Counting Money Received from The Phariya in Exchange for Rice
IX Pailas, Measuring Containers, Being Used for Bartering Commodities
X Scales Used for Weighing Green Vegetables
XI An Urban Trader Selling Mill-Made Clothes
XII An Urban Trader Selling Hubble Bubbles
XIII Lohras (Ironsmiths) Selling Their Implements
XIV Silversmiths with Their Jewelleries
XV Asur Women from Hills Selling Leaf Plates
XVI Mahli, Basket-Makers, Sitting with Their Trade Wares
XVII Birhor Women Selling Ropes and Wooden Tubs
XVIII Chik-Baraik, Weavers, Displaying Their Handloom Clothes
XIX Potters Occupying A Section of The Market Place
XX Valley Dwellers Chatting and Comparing Brooms Purchased at The Market Margins
XXI A Magician Amusing The Natives with Cobra, A Prelude to The Sale of His Magical Charms and Amulets
XXII The Tana Bhagats, A Reformist Sect of The Oraons, Holding A Meeting at The Market Margins
XXIII A Flute-Seller from Lohardaga
XXIV A Woman Selling Spices

CULTURE CHANGE IN AN INTERTRIBAL MARKET

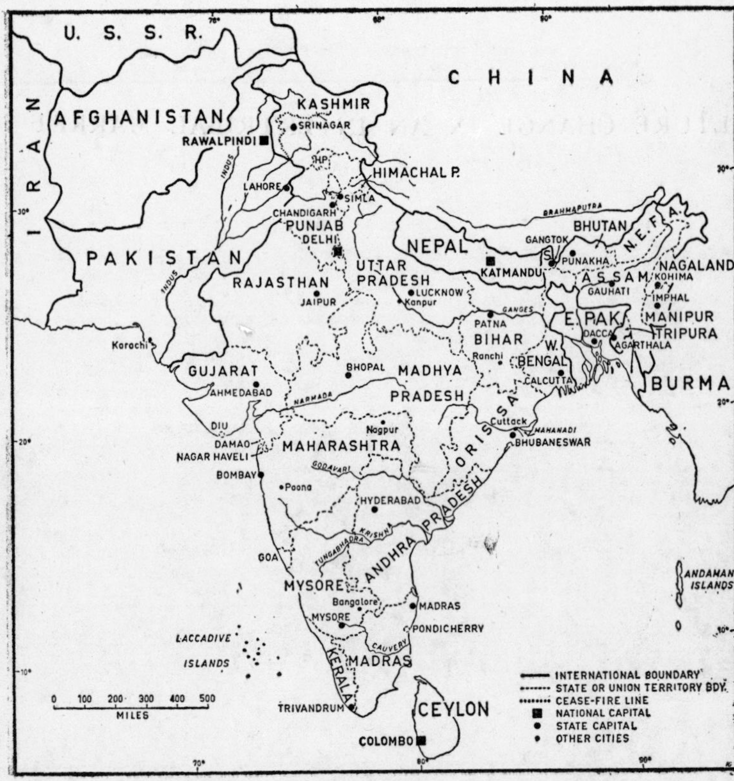

India Showing the State of Bihar

INTRODUCTION

In the revival of economic anthropology now current, the nature and functioning of markets is a key question both for ethnology and for the history and theory of social structure. In comparative sociology Indian social structure, with its distinctive interweaving of tribes, castes, cults, villages, village circles, and other institutions *sui generis* is a touchstone of variety in the structuring of human civilizations. Dr. Sinha has had the imagination to combine rich local colour, in fine strokes of detail of Indian up-country and tribal life, and good science, in the analysis and comparative importance of what he has seen.

The Banari market unfolded here is a small institution but a significant one. It is an open-country fair, a "cyclic market," assembling tribesmen, villager castemen, and city people, the "change-agents" of modernity carrying economic and governmental ties to the national horizon. It assembles these carriers of the significant and manifold diversities of Indian custom and institution not only in a drama of the economic exchange of the products of forest, field, and shop but also in a ritual enactment, well perceived and well understood by Dr. Sinha in his capacity (beyond his economist's role) of social and cultural analyst, reiterating the social structure in which tribes, castes, and the new national institutions all take part.

There is much interest today in social anthropology in the social functions of economic institutions and in the adaptation of institutions to ecological balance of human custom, resource, and diversity of terrain. The Banari intertribal market, remote and small as it is, shows well the mingling of economic and social functions and the integration of diverse groups of men and of their diverse terrains and resources which we have come to look for in social analysis of different national and regional institutions whether at the grass-roots level as here or at that of the Great Traditions—the classical monuments—of the world's peoples.

Like so many of the close-ups of the rich, raw data of ethnographic description which have yielded microcosms of society for anthropological comparison and interpretation, Dr. Sinha's Banari market reveals to us a *multum in parvo*. He shows us this multiplicity strand by strand. A country fair seemingly a clangour of colour and chaos becomes an ordered, ritual progression of human exchanges and social enactments of role and function. Centre of regional distribution of remote forest products of exotic and local kind with staples of village agriculture and modern necessities of urban and foreign provenance, hub of religious, social, and political communication, theatre of the culture changes of the region, where tribal meetings take place when dispersed forest dwellers find one another, where Hindu gods are newly proselytized to still animist people, where community development and public health officers dispense new worldwide agronomic or medical lore, the Banari market is much more than a market in any exclusively economic sense. Dr. Sinha shows it to be a dramatic enactment of the contacts of all the peoples of the region, an assemblage of the whole diversity of tribe, village, and outside institution in which cultural change is structured and channelled, particularly and specifically in the emergent *phariya's* or local culture-broker's role, in which a new figure has come to link inside and outside worlds in his own middleman's mediation of ancient tribal understandings with modern but here exotic institutional imperatives.

The Banari market is thus, one can hazard, something even of a microcosm of some of the oldest and most insistent (even most sympathetic) features of Indian social structure: diversity and simplicity retained side-by-side tolerantly interlaced always with complexity and modernity. As in Indian social structure, so in the market there is room, a niche, for every one ; there is always a place on the fair-ground for him and always some mediator or other to link him with all the others. The Banari market preserves, for a time anyway, indeed it expresses, the balanced specialization of the dispersed forest hamlets of the Mundas and Dravidians and the centering villages of the Hindus. The balance of specialization and centering functions—of collecting and cultivating—is not only a symbiosis of man in the valleys and plateaus of the Chota Nagpur Hills, it is also a climax structure of social organizational complexities, with the simplest-organized monkey-hunters at the margins and the complex, multicaste Hindu village at the valley center. Dr. Sinha can rightly see that this little country fair that here still in India assembles periodically, at one node of a much wider market network of similar cyclical assemblages, the dispersed castes and tribes settled across the forest-and-valley landscape for hundreds of miles, much as once elsewhere similar fairs and markets drew together other landscapes in West Africa or Europe or Japan, prototypes of social structure organized by open network rather than by closed, compartmented, cell-like unities as in the walled city-societies of Middle-Eastern and classical traditions usually relied-on for models of the social structure of emergent civilizations.

Functionally, thus, Dr. Sinha can conclude rightly enough that this little fair, both market and ceremony, "maintains a network of socio-cultural ties among the peoples of its hinterland" and gives them thus "a common base for their regional ethnology."

Structurally, however, the Banari market teaches much more. Most interesting indeed is the detail we get here on the coincidence of the form of the market itself and the network structure of its society, even by implication, at least by guess, of Indian civilization itself. The spacings, the positions, the roles played in each market day, of tribesmen, castemen, and outsiders, are revealing in the extreme. Shy tribals at the periphery, city-contacts at the centre, locals ranging between as *phariyas* (culturebrokers, middlemen), the very lay-out of the fair is a replication of an "ethnic mosaic," a joining of many cultures. But it is a much different mosaic than that of Middle-Eastern nomads, peasants, mountaineers, and artisans, different even from that of the multicaste villages of the North Indian plain.

Ethnological and social structural implications can thus be drawn from this study of the rustic Banari market and its hinterland ranging far beyond the correct but modest conclusions largely functional in nature with which Dr. Sinha has wisely contented himself. Thus the mosaic of tribes and castes, peripheral hamlets and nucleated villages making up the local region can be offered as an excellent candidate for a guess as to the earlier structuring of the cultural unification of ethnic, religious, and linguistic diversities achieved in Indian society. In this region the marginality of the forests, the centralizing force of the village rice lands still strike an ecological balance of dispersions and concentrations in a population not yet thick on the land and in a climate not requiring central control, where it was forest gatherers, tropical gardeners, and peasant, intensive cultivators who made a division of labour rather than such other specializations as went into other civilizations. There is an old strain of explanation of the Indian caste system as a drawing together of tribes short of dissolving them and an old appeal to jungle and warm climate as sparers, along with congruent religious and philosophical tolerance, of differences and refuges that is borne out here.

Symbiosis and dispersion, ecological specialization and economic integration, are general forces. They are not precise enough in themselves to account for specific cultural emergence, or as here, for the caste system of India and the "rural cosmopolitanism" that has made Indian civilization so different from the urban and imperial integrations seen in other histories (Mediterranean and Chinese, for example). The specific details of culture and civilization of India have their own history and have other parallels (European, never imperially centralized, only latterly urbanized, Japanese, Polynesian, African, etc.). For them the emergence and endurance of a social organization using the open-country fair rather than the city bazaar as a central mechanism of exchange, assemblage, and integration, like the special historical Indian forces of polytheism and monasticism, needs careful and informed comparative historical and institutional investigation. India never was simply only an overflow from the Middle-Eastern civilization of cities, empires, and congregational religions and she needs well to be recognized for her own historical institutional evolutions and inventions.

Another specific inference, this time for economic anthropology rather than for comparative sociology, is the intriguing local coexistence of customs about moneys (media of exchange). Dr. Sinha's Banari market documents well the difference between money as equivalences of traditional commodities and "all-purpose" money serving as medium of exchange. Along with mnemonic valuables, or money as standard of payment of the obligations of reciprocities, these two "money uses" were the three kinds or stages of money hypothesized from economic history and anthropology by Karl Polanyi[1] and demonstrated by him to mark the institutional symbol-systems (that is, the variant kinds of money) developed in societies organized economically as systems respectively or reciprocal exchange, of redistribution, and of markets. Without burdening Dr. Sinha's findings with the polemic about the real existence of these asserted three alternative economic systems and their broadening of economic theory from formal, Western economics to "substantive" inductive discovery of non-Western economic principles evolved in other cultures than those habituated to the market system of the West, it is good to note this empirical vindication of a Polanyi thesis. Dr. Sinha reports quite explicity the presence at his market of both old tribal equivalences and the new "all-purpose" or universal money. We see money refused by tribals in favor of fixed conversions of staple for staple and we see the new *phariyas,* the Hindu culture-brokers, about whom Dr. Sinha has written so well elsewhere, specifically mediating exchanges of goods for goods for final conversion to money prices. Indeed we get here an intimate and eloquent detailing of the very arrival of money as a concept and an institution. The new medium of exchange and its adherent customs and understandings, the new fluctuations of price and the new generality of convertibility dawn here before our eyes, in the contacts of the city-contacts over the *phariyas* with the astonished local tribals, just as freshly as do the other piquant novelties of the national state and the modern world: postal service, individual taxes, advertising, voting and electioneering, etc.

Indeed, lastly, the Baṇari market, like any central ceremony of a culture, is also a channel of cultural and social change, and Dr. Sinha has not neglected to show us well how that change takes place. Westernization, Sanskritization, national integration are lively currents of modern Indian life,

[1] Polanyi, Karl, Conrad M. Arensberg and Harry W. Pearson. *Trade and Market in the Early Empires*, Glencoe, Illinois : The Free Press and The Falcon's Wing Press, 1957.

and much studied by Indian and foreign scholars alike. In the tribal and village contact here depicted they get a very special and a very illuminating exemplification. It is not only in consumption habits or in changes of attitude that such change takes place; it is also in the arrival of new personnel with new roles in new institutions that the contact with the older custom is effected and the transformation, at least the addition, the superposition, of the new ways goes forward. Dr. Sinha is very careful with his elucidation for us of the persons and the behaviors of the change-agents who take their places each Monday at the roadside on the fair-grounds by the booths of the city-traders who descend from the bus on the new all-weather road there. Like the traders they too meet then and there, with their new wares and new messages, the tribesmen and castemen of the old traditions still assembling as before for buying and selling, for communing and socializing and conducting tribe and caste business; for fun and for courting and for news. The very listing of them as they take their central places on the fair-grounds gives the institutional inclusions of Indian life, old and new, into which the remote region is being swept, and their presence and action at the fair show the changes which they lead: the Hindu-Rajput landlord of the village lands (a new and sole figure, but certainly one common in the greater India outside), the market-side Hindu temple, with Brahman officiant, (likewise a figure new here, but old and still Sanskritizing the tribals as through centuries), the Christian missionary, the postman, the tax-collector, the community-development officer, the political-party campaigner, the nostrum-advertizer, even the anthropologist.

Columbia University CONRAD M. ARENSBERG

CHAPTER I

THE PROBLEM

I

THE basic objective of the present study is to describe, analyse, and interpret the institution of the Banari intertribal market located in the Chota Nagpur hills of Bihar, India, as an agent of culture change.

Chota Nagpur (see Map II), an area of about twenty-six thousand square miles, is the homeland of over three million tribal people, comprising some two dozen tribal groups. Most tribal groups occupy habitats exclusively among themselves though some share these with peasant Hindus. A few tribal groups, though living in discrete settlements, have frequent contact with neighbouring tribal or peasant communities. Monographs on the Chota Nagpur tribal groups include those by Roy 1912 ; 1915 ; 1925 ; 1928 ; 1937 ; Majumdar 1937 ; 1950 ; Dalton 1872 ; Leuva 1962 ; but all of these writers have treated the tribal groups as if they were isolated. In other words, anthropological studies in this culture area have thus far over-emphasized isolation of tribal communities and underemphasized interrelationships among the various tribes. Perhaps this has been in part due to the anthropological tradition of studying so-called self-contained simple societies.

The present study emerged from the belief that truly isolated communities are, in most instances, non-existent, and also from the opinion that anthropologists have a responsibility to report the precise channels by which communities have established relationships—such as economic, political, or social—with one another and with the larger society. In the past, such channels have often been ignored in favour of relationships which function mostly within a community.

This study, however, is concerned not with a community as such but rather with the institution of a weekly market, which serves to bring together members of a number of communities from a well-defined territory to participate in activities signi-

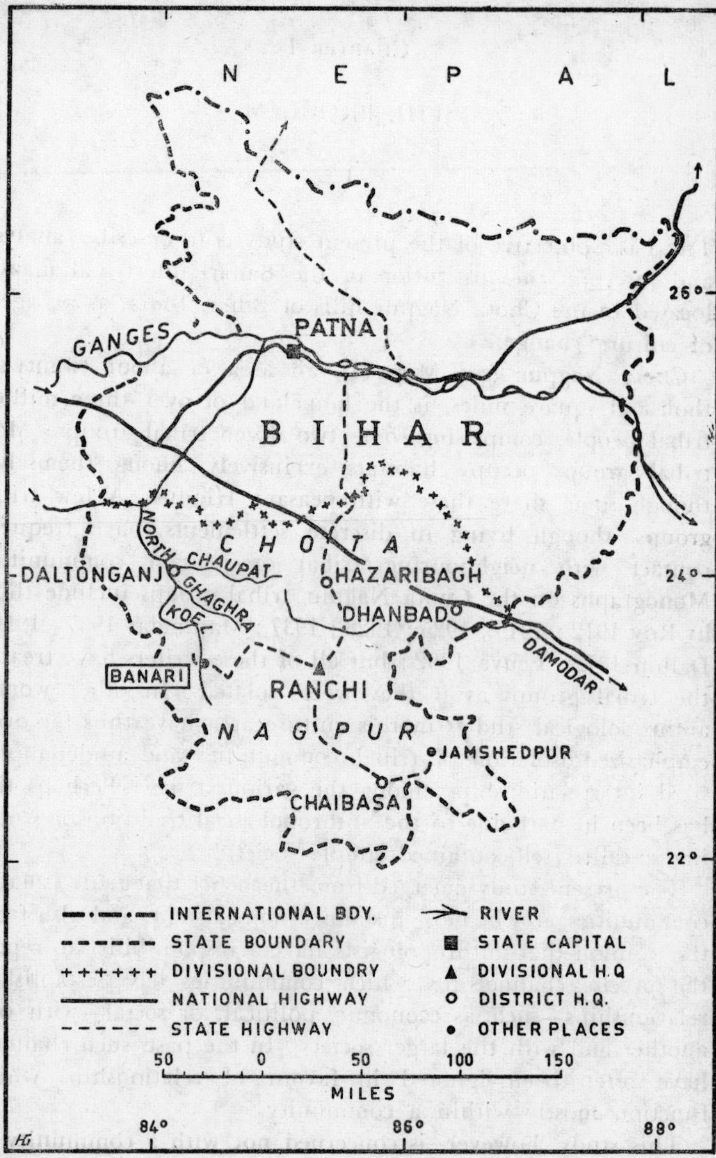

Chota Nagpur in Bihar State showing the Banari Region.

fying interdependence rather than independence, and extension rather than isolation, of the people who take part.

A market has been conceptualized in several ways. It may just mean a business place, a specific site where a group of buyers and a group of sellers meet. It may refer, as in economic parlance, to the intangible principle which determines prices through the interplay of forces of supply and demand, irrespective of the site of transactions. It may be viewed geographically as a physical unit of territory, or it may be viewed socially as a more or less structured group of individuals whose bids and offers reflect the supply and demand situation and thereby establish the price (Encyclopaedia of the Social Sciences 1933 : 10 : 131).

To the anthropologist interested in interacting patterns of human behaviour, however, a market has more than economic, geographic, or social significance. For understanding the full cultural dimensions of a market, the social, religious, political, and other cultural factors are also important. Recognition of these factors becomes more significant as we move from examining a highly complex economy to the economy of simple societies. In such societies, the economic behaviour is conditioned more directly by social and other cultural patterns of the people than is true of complex societies. Sometimes it is difficult to distinguish between purely economic and purely socio-cultural behaviour.

This difficulty denies the neat working of economic laws and makes the market situation rather complicated, warranting a fresh inquiry of such markets from an extra-economic, multi-dimensional perspective. It may be noted that the actual territorial dimension of a market does not end with its market place, but it extends beyond, to the land and the people comprising the geographical and cultural regions served by the market. Any anthropological inquiry of a market must consider all contributing factors.

This report is an anthropological study of an intertribal market as a social phenomenon as distinguished from a purely economic consideration of such an institution. The intertribal market is conceived as one of the major institutions binding together various communities, not only economically but socially, politically, and otherwise, as well. By focusing attention on an institution significantly involving several communities, the present study must of necessity delineate the characteristics of the individual communities as well as the network of relationships among them. In one way this study may contribute significantly to the understanding of the ethnology of the region of the intertribal market; in another the study may provide an appropriate context in which to analyse and understand cultural and intercultural processes in the region.

The present study is a holistic analysis of an intertribal market at Banari in the heart of the Chota Nagpur hills. The writer has tried to relate the market system as a whole to the wider context of the ecological and cultural patterns of the region and to show the functional relationships between economic and social, political, and other cultural patterns of the region.

II

There have been very few studies of markets, for example, Bohannan and others, in tribal communities, and still fewer of the socio-cultural implications of an intertribal market. It is worthwhile to review some of the outstanding works in related fields by anthropologists.

The earliest definitive works were by Boas (1898), Thurnwald (1932), and Malinowski (1926); they were primarily concerned with primitive economics or economic anthropology. These works considered economic motivations as integral parts of social process but did not chart their role in intertribal or intercultural spheres. Malinowski's discriminating study of the Trobriand islanders was the first account to bring out some socio-cultural ramifications of economic activities. He showed how the production of goods and services was conditioned by political, religious, social, and kinship institutions among the Trobriand islanders. Exchange of gifts, ceremonial distribution of goods, and barter outside the tribe all had social, ritualistic, and political significance. Later, works by Ruth Benedict (1934) and Margaret Mead (1937), though proceeding from a different methodological base than Malinowski's, confirmed his results. A different, but equally important, innovation in this field was made by Thurnwald (1932) who pointed out, on the basis of his ethnological studies in East Africa, that social stratification usually results from cultural contacts between occupationally specialized communities. Although Thurnwald's theory basically was related to the theory of economic development, he placed great stress on gift-giving or reciprocity as a pervasive element in tribal economic life, a pattern far removed from the acquisitive motives of the modern self-regulating market economy.

During the last two decades there has been considerable interest in the study of primitive economies. These studies have used concepts of modern economics indiscriminately, and the results of this borrowing have not been entirely profitable. Although the studies by Malinowski, Mead, and Thurnwald had certain limitations, they showed an awareness of the social context of distribution, pointed out the socio-cultural motives involved, and treated economic life as a part of the total web of life of the tribal community. But later anthropologists, anxious to use concepts from contemporary economic theories, attempted to cast anthropological data in the frame of modern economics, yielding a net result of pseudo-anthropology and pseudo-economics. Herskovits' *Economic Anthropology* (1952) is the best example of how empirical knowledge of primitive economics was misplaced within the framework of orthodox economic theory. He treated topics such as production, distribution, exchange, property, and economic surplus, a scheme reminiscent of classical economists.

Sol Tax (1953) likewise described the typical Guatemalan village as a perfect example of strong market economy, "a money economy . . . with a strongly developed market which tends to be perfectly competitive" (pp. 11-13). But his descriptive details hardly supported his characterization. The institutional basis of the market economy and the tremendous differences between market and non-market institutional patterns were not clearly delineated. In his Guatemalan village, for example, land can be transferred, but its sale is restricted by the traditional attitude that it must be preserved for the family. There is no true labour market, for few free and landless workers are found. And, there hardly exists a "capital market" although loans are occasionally made for consumption goods. A weakness of Tax's account appears when he accepted a conceptual framework of modern economic theory and then cast his data accordingly. Another important study is that of D. M. Goodfellow (1939) who argued that the concepts of economic theory have universal validity, although he treated four Bantu economies as self-contained entities.

More satisfactory treatments of peasant economies within modern economic theory are those of Raymond Firth. In his study of Tikopia (1939), Firth used concepts of economic theory primarily to show that the Polynesian is both realistic and rational in his economic life rather than as a framework within which to analyse the economy. However, when his data reflected economic theory, as is the case of the Malayan fishing economy (1946), he used them with great profit. But Firth, because he recognized that his data were limited, did not explore the relationship between fishing activities and other aspects of socio-cultural life in the community.

More recently, Dewey (1962) and Bohannan and Dalton (1962) have presented interesting data on tribal and peasant markets. Dewey's ethnography of a peasant market in Java, generally excellent, ignored the socio-cultural implications of a market as an institution, however. Her treatment was more economic than cultural, and like most economists, her analysis was segmental rather than holistic. The Bohannan-Dalton volume contained various papers cast in a strictly economic frame for socio-economic context, but the volume is a definite contribution to the understanding of the nature of markets in different types of economies. As their study was aimed at a classification of primitive African economies on the basis of market and marketless communities, it discussed the form rather than functions of the markets; the studies ignored to a great extent socio-cultural ramifications of tribal marketing.

Use of the concepts of economic theory offers only limited advantages to anthropologists. It focuses attention on the problems of alternatives and choice, but it often interferes with the institutional analysis emphasized in anthropological studies. Unlike economists, anthropologists, whose approach is holistic and multi-dimensional, strive to develop a broader theoretical scheme, broad enough to cover both the modern market economy and the economies of tribal people, in which the formal economies of the market appear only as aspects of the totality.

Very notable collaboration between economists and anthropologists has produced an excellent treatise on *Trade and Market in the Early Empires* (Polanyi, Arensberg and Pearson 1957). Here the contributors have examined "market place" and "marketless" economies in history and society where there is little "economizing," that is, little economic framework to compel the individual to "rational" and "efficient" economic activity or "optimum" allocation of his resources. They suggested that in such cases the economy should not be subject to *economic* analysis but to *institutional* analysis (p. 357). Polanyi and his associates made very useful distinction between the modern "self-regulating market" and the "market place" and provided excellent leads for understanding and analysis of marketing in so-called "market place" and "marketless" societies.

By studying one intertribal market, Banari, in the institutional context on a microcosmic level, the present study may provide significant leads—methodological and theoretical—for understanding the complex socio-economic processes of cultural continuity and change with which anthropology has long been concerned.

III

The following formulations are explicit hypotheses for the present study.

1. An intertribal market provides a meeting place for economic and cultural specialists of different tribes and is a centre for not only economic but also social, religious, and political activity in the region.

2. An intertribal market helps to create and maintain a network of socio-cultural ties among the peoples of its hinterland, thus providing a common base for regional ethnology.

3. An intertribal market serves as an agent of culture change in the region. Through its various socio-economic processes, it brings about culture change among the primitive and the folk cultures of the region.

Chapter II

APPROACH TO THE STUDY OF THE BANARI INTERTRIBAL MARKET

I

This study is based on empirical findings, both diachronic and synchronic, regarding a weekly intertribal market at Banari in Bihar, central India. The field-work was carried out at Banari and throughout its hinterland during the period between the autumn of 1957 and the spring of 1961. In so far as the field-work was conducted in different seasons of these years, a continuity was maintained for nearly forty months.

A word must be said at the outset regarding the selections of the Banari intertribal market for intensive, microcosmic study. Numerous intertribal markets were on the Chota Nagput plateaus, and the Banari market was one of the most interior of these. It was located at the terminus of a surfaced road which had been in use only during the past decade. Hence it provided a rather ideal laboratory for investigating the traditional role of the market amidst modern forces of acculturation and culture change. The investigator's familiarity with the region, acquired while doing earlier enthnographic work among Birhor, a semi-nomadic community, also influenced the selections of the Banari market. Recognition of both the area and the topic as relatively little known provided added stimuli for selecting Banari.

The field research on this intertribal market was primarily divided into three aspects, although these did not follow any sequential order.

1. First, the investigator made an intensive study of the Banari intertribal market, *in situ*. It was in this phase (1957-58) that the local ethnographic data were collected, the spatial distribution of commodities was charted, the socio-cultural affinity of people attending the market was recorded, and the nature of contacts with people, insti-

tutions, and organizations belonging to the urban centres was evaluated.

2. In the second portion of the research the investigator extended his field study to the hinterland, working among people of different communities attending this intertribal market. He studied the people's preparation for attending the market, travelled with them, and observed their patterns of behaviour in the market place, and then returned with them again to their village, in order to understand the full effects of marketing on their lives. This procedure was followed for each of the major tribal communities in the hinterland at least a dozen times during 1958. It also resulted in a clear understanding of the ecological and cultural patterns of the hinterland and also of their inter-relationship with the market.
3. The third phase included a study of seasonal changes in the structure and composition of the market and the correlated changes in the hinterland. This was done by returning to the Banari intertribal market and its hinterland six times for a period of six weeks each during 1958 and 1959. On several occasions the writer followed the itinerary of the urban traders to smaller tributary markets in the peripheries of the hinterland. An extensive study of five such markets helped in defining the position of the Banari intertribal market vis-a-vis the tributary markets and analysing the network of socio-cultural ties in the hinterland and outside. It also provided comparative material for the study of markets elsewhere in the region.

II

In the present study, observation, interview, participation, and case study were all used in various phases of collecting the field data. Observation provided basic information and insights into the workings of the institution of the intertribal market, for example, the layout of the market place and the kind of explicit socio-cultural and economic interactions among the peoples attending it. This provided leads for subsequent interviews. Interviews were generally unstructured but were directed enough to yield pertinent information. Interviews were conducted both at the market place and in the villages of the hinterland. Sometimes urban traders were interviewed before and after the market period. On many occasions the investigator participated in the market activities as a buyer, as an agent-friend of the landlord, as a member of the audience in political and religious rallies, and also once as an assistant to a middle man. This gave an inside view of marketing procedures. Several case studies of urban influences exerted through the market upon the hinterland were made, especially of a few technological innovations, introduction of all-purpose money, and community development programmes for the tribal areas which were initiated by the government.

Library research provided ethnological, geological, zoological, botanical, and geographical material on the hinterland and was of great assistance in rechecking and supplementing the field data. It should also be mentioned that the use of native dialects, Dravidian Kurukh and Indo-Aryan Sadani, in the interviews greatly facilitated the field-work.

CHAPTER III

ECOLOGICAL SETTING OF THE BANARI INTERTRIBAL MARKET

I

THE Banari intertribal market serves an area of 494 square miles in the Chota Nagpur peneplains of central India. This area, the hinterland of the intertribal market, was demarcated in the autumn of 1958 by mapping the distance trekked by natives attending the weekly market. On the basis of a survey during five successive market days, it was found that the north-south extension of the hinterland had a maximum distance of twenty-six miles and the east-west extension ranged nineteen miles (see Map III).

The hinterland served by the Banari market included territories from three parganas, revenue divisions of Chota Nagpur, namely, Bhitarbarwe, Kasmar, and Chechari. All three parganas are dissected by hills and streams : hills with flat tops or pointed peaks, sometimes barren, sometimes forested ; and streams which are perennial or seasonal, wide or narrow, differing appreciably from one another.

The network of rivers and streams which dissects the region would appear to impede rather than facilitate movements of people, and there is a virtual absence of effective communication in the hinterland. Many settlements on the hills and plateaus are inaccessible. Only those who live there find it worthwhile to undertake the arduous trip to the market each week. The rugged terrain, with its broken hills and numerous water courses, makes communication difficult, especially in the monsoon season, between hills and plateaus, the ecological margins, and the valley, the ecological centre of the region.

In 1781, when British authorities surveyed the country and then published *Rennel's Map of Hindostan,* this region of the Chota Nagpur plains was not included. The survey was carried out only as far as Adar, a village which stands in the south-eastern corner of the region. Perhaps the inaccessibility of

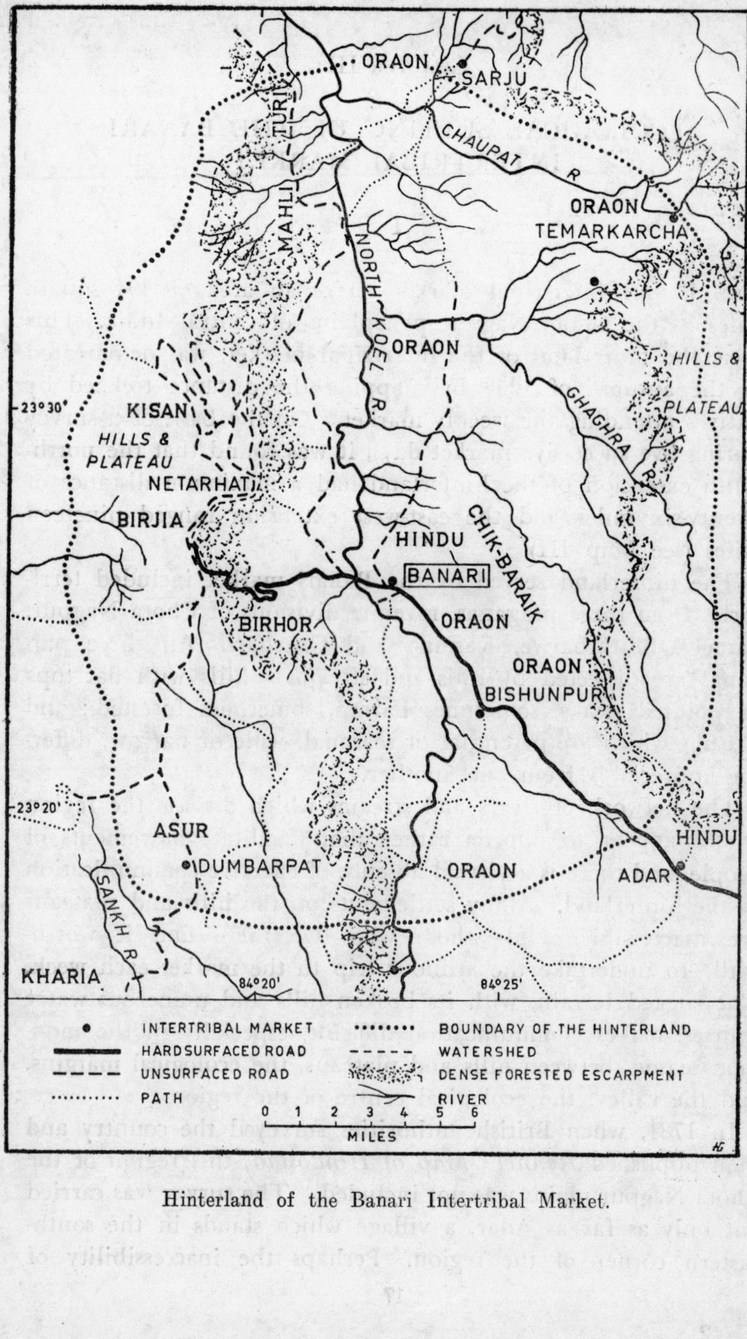

Hinterland of the Banari Intertribal Market.

the region prevented its survey. Until 1916, this region was not connected to the outside world, even by cart track. It was only then that an unsurfaced road was built to connect Banari to Lohardaga, forty miles south-east, the terminus of a narrow-gauge railroad in Chota Nagpur. In 1931, the cart track was extended westward from Banari to a village called Morwai, at the foothills of the ecological margins of the region. A mule track connected the valley to the hills and plateaus.

During the 1930's, a cart track was made to connect Banari with the northern border of the hinterland, as far as a market place called Sarju. Another cart track was built along the North Koel River to Garo, an intertribal market in the north. A third track connected Banari to its southern limit, the Tendar intertribal market. All these unpaved roads connected outlying settlements to the valley, linking Banari to them as spokes leading into the hub of a wheel; most hill and plateau settlements, however, remained isolated literally from one another.

The network of rough roads in the valley was built more for facilitating administration than for bringing the natives into regular communication with the outside world. Few public vehicles plied these roads. However, in the 1940's, when the government extended its forest conservation policies, thus including the Banari region, roads were laid, and the region was opened to outsiders, contractors, and officials. Still, as the roads were workable only during fair weather, the outside world and its affairs hardly penetrated the isolation of the natives. The natives continued to use the paths and tracks to which they were accustomed, mostly carrying their loads on their shoulders. Few people used pack animals in the region, and hardly any carts were seen on the hills and plateaus. Even in the valley there were hardly any carts owned by natives. Some Hindu traders, who attended the weekly Banari intertribal market, coming from Ghaghra and Lohardaga, eighteen and forty miles away, respectively, to the south, used ponies and bullock carts for their journey.

In the year 1943, a private agency started a bus service from Lohardaga to Banari; because the roads were bad and the vehicles old, however, the service was very irregular. However, in 1947, the road was surfaced; streams and rivers were bridged;

and a new bus service connected the Banari region once daily with Lohardaga and the outside world. By 1958 another bus was added, and service continued without interruption.

Since 1947, after India's independence, the State Government of Bihar showed special interest in the Banari region. Special community development programmes were introduced in tribal areas, and forest resources were exploited on a greater scale than before, opening up the region for large-scale contacts from the outside world. Within the region, however, the ecological relationship between the valley and the hills and plateaus, although not undisturbed, hardly lost its internal balance. The Banari intertribal market served as a shield for the region against mass communication with the outside world on the one hand, and as a filter of influence to the hinterland from the outside on the other, thereby contributing to the continuance of the ecological balance of the region.

II

The hinterland served by the Banari intertribal market comprises two distinct ecological zones. The hills and plateaus comprise the first ecological zone, which is characterized by rocky upland with small, scattered deposits of iron ore; the escarpments and slopes are marked by dry forest interspersed by luxuriant growth of wild trees, bamboos, and other fibrous plants. The second of these is the valley, the nucleus of the hinterland; it is dominated by the fertile affluence of the North Koel River and is dissected by numerous small streams emerging from the surrounding hills and plateaus. The elevation of the hills and plateaus goes up to 3,700 feet, which is, incidentally, the highest point in Chota Nagpur, and the valley, the centre of the region, has an average altitude of 2,100 feet. Close observation of the ecological characteristics of the region leads one to think of the hills and plateaus as the margins, and the valley as the centre, of the hinterland of the Banari intertribal market.

III

Although the region falls within tropical climatic conditions, there is internal variation between the ecological margins and its centre which in turn is reflected in the relationship the intertribal market has with the margins and the centre. The following tables present comparative data on rainfall (Table 1) and temperature (Table 2) at the ecological margins and centre of the region for the year 1959.

In spite of the impressive record of rainfall in the region, rain has not been of much actual value to the people in their agricultural efforts. Failure of rain in August-September means famine on the ecological margins where the drainage pattern is such that the advantages of a plentiful rainfall are almost negligible. Drought conditions, together with the infertile and rocky lands, make life hard for the few tribal inhabitants of these marginal areas. Almost alone, the rainfall determines the economic lot of people in the ecological margins. A settlement officer once described this region as "probably the area which is least able to resist conditions of scarcity" (Reid 1908 : 6).

Rainfall data for the ecological margins and centre of the region indicate that monsoon rains generally break in June and continue through October, although occasional showers appear in other months of the year. Except for a few places where water can be naturally stored (though it invariably dries up during the summer), there is always a paucity of water on the ecological margins. On the other hand, the centre of the region harvests maximum benefit from the monsoon—through rivers, good drainage, and internal underground saturation.

There is no great difference in the temperature between the ecological margins and centre of the region ; however, higher elevation in the margins reduces the humidity in summer.

In the hinterland, the natives distinguish three seasons in a yearly cycle ; they are summer, monsoon, and winter. Those who till lands prepare their fields in summer, sow them during the monsoon, and harvest their crop in winter. For the artisan groups, winter and summer are the productive seasons ; the monsoons confine them indoors, forcing them to depend solely on stored raw materials. The seasonal variation in the region is also reflected in the extent of activities at the market place. During the monsoon, when communication is seriously diminished by rains, one sees very little activity at the market

Table 1

RAINFALL 1959 IN MILLIMETRE

	Jan.	Feb.	Mar.	Apr.	May	June	July	Aug.	Sept.	Oct.	Nov.	Dec.
Ecological Margins	60.8	2.6	6.0	8.6	39.0	144.2	233.6	363.0	506.6	187.5	0	0
Ecological Centre	68.8	8.0	1.2	16.6	39.6	278.6	628.0	537.8	513.2	224.6	0	0

Table 2

TEMPERATURE 1959 IN FAHRENHEIT

	Jan.	Feb.	Mar.	Apr.	May	June	July	Aug.	Sept.	Oct.	Nov.	Dec.
Ecological Margins	53.26	53.28	58.25	63.36	67.58	72.63	71.87	72.32	75.86	69.82	55.36	49.61
Ecological Centre	59.93	62.25	74.29	80.9	85.22	81.23	73.54	74.03	74.66	71.34	67.23	57.87

place. More specially, the participation of men and the appearance of material from the ecological margins decline. Winter is the busiest season for the market, and summer ranks next. In both seasons, continuous interaction among peoples from the margins and the centre exists.

IV. The Ecological Margins : Hills and Plateaus

A projective profile of the Chota Nagpur peneplains provides a visual image of the nature of the hills and plateaus constituting the ecological margins of the hinterland. The hills of the region are mostly broken ; sometimes they have level tops like plateaus, and, in other cases, they have a regular rise and fall in elevation. But all of them finally disappear into the valley, the ecological centre of the region. In some areas of the region, hills form a circular basin with a narrow outlet, as at Chechari. In this isolated basin, millet is produced ; the basin is inhabited by the Kisan, a tribe which plays a special role at the intertribal market.

For the most part, however, the hills are topped with undulating plains. The ranges to the west of Banari, running along the North Koel River, are of this kind. The undulating plateau is a rocky upland, varying in density of forest and dispersed human habitation. The hills are formed geologically by great masses of laterite, sandstone trip, and crystalline rocks which have considerable iron ore deposits (Singh 1958 : 25). The tribal people living on the plateaus have long known ways of smelting iron ores for making crude implements which find their way to the Banari intertribal market. Most of the hills are relatively inaccessible, but one can observe from the valley several clearings on the hillsides where natives raise maize, using, until recently, the techniques of shifting cultivation. Maize constitutes an important commodity at the Banari intertribal market.

A vast forest belt, part of the ecological margins of the hinterland, stands between the hills and the valley. On the hills, as well as in the valley, however, wild forests have been gradually disappearing. Unscrupulous methods of shifting cultivation and haphazard use of wood for smelting iron have deforested the hills and, in the valley, the clearing of the forests for cultivation has led to further denudation. Notwithstanding these losses, the Banari forest range still constitutes an important forest reserve in Chota Nagpur. Some tribes, as will be seen in the next chapter, make their living from the forests; their traditional ways have contributed both to the exploitation and the conservation of these forests.

The forests contribute to the Banari intertribal market in distinctive ways. The local forests are of the dry, deciduous variety. Their most important species is *Shorea robusta,* locally known as Sāl, which comprises over half the forest. The Sāl trees are generally found in depressions along the banks of streams and rivulets and on the slopes of hills. Big trees are scarce; the bulk of them are in the pole stage and mostly of coppice origin. The Sāl provides natives with wood for building houses, and material for making ploughs and various other implements which one finds at the market. Some tribal settlers of the region, like the Birhor, manufacture wooden tubs from Sāl wood and sell them in the market. They also collect the fruit of this tree, for consumption and exchange in the market. Other tribes, like the Asurs, use Sāl leaves for making native cups and plates which are sold at the market.

In the Sāl forests, other varieties of trees are also found: *Buchanania latifolia,* locally known as Biar and *Anogeissos latifolia* known as Dhauntia, are other fruit-bearing trees, the fruits of which the natives collect and consume or sell at the market. *Acacia catechu,* Khair, which provides a chewing substance, is popular among people in different parts of India, providing the natives with a marketable commodity. The fruits of *Phyuanthus emblica,* Aura, have medicinal value, and native doctor's booths at the market find place for them.

The mixed forests of bamboos and other trees which constitute the remaining portion of the forested hinterland are of greater importance to the natives than the Sāl forests—insofar as they provide several marketable commodities. Bamboo is the basic material for making baskets, combs, sticks, flutes, containers, and several other commodities widely used in the hinterland. The Māhlis, an artisan tribe, make their living by marketing these commodities. *Bassia latifolia,* Mahua, bears flowers which are collected by the natives and fermented as a native beer, which also enters the market. Trees like Bāir,

Paras, and Kusum bear lac, which is a cash crop and an export commodity for the natives. Some wild trees provide oil seeds which natives collect, press, and consume, or sell at the market.

Apart from these forest trees, there are some creepers such as *Bahenia Scandens,* Chop, which provide raw material for making strings and ropes. A semi-nomadic community, Birhor, specializes in manufacturing ropes, from which its inhabitants make their living. The forest also provides some vegetable roots and new shoots of bamboos which the natives consume and sometimes, during periods of scarcity, sell at the market. Even leaves of *Phoenix cylvestris,* date palms, are collected by the natives, who weave mats from them and sell them in the market. Some natives collect honey from the forest for sale at the market.

The forested part of the hinterland contains many wild animals, such as leopards, bears, boars, deer, bisons, and monkeys. In the north-west corner of the region one often encounters wild elephants. Smaller animals, such as foxes, hares, porcupines, and various fowls, are innumerable, and they provide delicacies for the natives. Of these animals, many of which are hunted and eaten by the natives, only monkeys become a marketable commodity. The Birhors specialize in monkey-trapping. Until recently they feasted on monkey meat, and sold the skins at the market for use by the tribes of the regions in making drums. However, they now export live monkeys, through agents at the intertribal market, to rhesus experimental centre and scientific laboratories.

V. The Ecological Centre : The Valley

From the above description of the ecological margins of the hinterland, it is apparent that they are utilized in multifarious ways, and the tribes furnish a variety of commodities to the intertribal market. While these observations are true, it should be noted, however, that the extent of influence of the marginal areas is limited in terms of total volume of commodities handled at the market. It is the valley, the ecological centre of the region, which provides the important goods and services to the hinterland.

The ecological centre lies essentially in the fertile valley of the North Koel River. Almost 82 per cent of the population of the hinterland live in and on the resources of this valley. The ecologically favourable situation accounts for the nucleated settlement pattern of the valley and perhaps also for the choice of Banari as the locus of the intertribal market.

Of the 3.1 million acres of land in the hinterland, only one-sixtieth or about 50,000 acres are cultivable. Although statistics are not available, an estimated area of 25,000 acres remain uncultivated wasteland every year. Eighty-five per cent of the cultivated land lies in the valley, but due to topographical features of the valley it is not equally productive.

There are primarily two varieties of arable lands, locally known as Don and Tanr. Don is the terraced lowland, almost quadrangular in shape, ranging from one-eighth to a half acre in area, and is more fertile than the latter. The edges of the terraced plot are raised twelve to eighteen inches, with mud on the three sides. The fourth, on the upper side of the parcel, is kept open for allowing a flow of water inside the field. The Don lands are generally found beside rivers and streams. It may be noted that there is a conspicuous absence of Don lands on hills and plateaus of the region. From the point of view of fertility, Don lands are more productive, but at the same time they are divided into two categories called Choura Don and Garha Don. Choura Don constitutes those plots of lowlands which do not retain water for long but receive it in plenty during monsoon. On the other hand, Garha Don consists of those lands which retain water throughout the whole year. However, such lands are very limited in the valley.

Both types of Don lands yield the most important crop, rice, of the hinterland. The Garha Don produces fine grain rice and its yield is twice that of the Choura Don. Sometimes Choura Don is also used for cultivating lentils, gram, and barley.

The Tanr lands, which vary from 80 to 90 per cent of the cultivable land of the region, are uplands. Parcels of this land may be as large as ten acres, but they yield poor crops. They are dry lands; they retain little water or moisture; and if not properly cared for, they become barren and infertile.

On the basis of soil type, Tanr lands are of three kinds: one, Rugri Tanr, those fields which are strong and sloping without any depth of soil ; two, Nagra Tanr, which have hard, dark soil ; and third, Khirsi Tanr, which have red soil. The third type is the best ; it produces wheat, gram, barley, and paddy. The second produces various kinds of lentils and grams ; the first produces wild rice and millet.

The tribal groups living in the valley depend on these lands wholly or partially for their subsistence. Rice is both a staple and cash crop. It constitutes an important commodity at the market. Other crops are raised for home, or local, consumption, and they appear at the market only infrequently.

Some natives raise vegetables : squash, tomatoes, potatoes, egg-plant, and pumpkin, in the kitchen garden. They exchange or sell these at the market.

In contrast to the ecological margins, where one finds very few domesticated animals, every family in the ecological centre raises cattle, pigs, and poultry. Cattle are generally used in ploughing, cows provide milk and clarified butter (the latter is sold at the market to Hindu peasants) ; pigs provide meat and also bring cash ; and poultry constitutes the most handy commodity for trade at the market. Eggs are also traded. The natives buy pigs and poultry for feasts, ceremonies, and rituals. Goats are also raised in the valley, and along with pigs, their meat is sold every week at the market place. The hides of cattle and goats make export-commodities and are traded to urban traders at the market place.

VI

The foregoing description of the hinterland served by the Banari intertribal market in terms of the ecological margins and centre brings out an interesting point : there is a distinct pattern of relationship between climate, flora, fauna, and human beings in the ecological margins and in the ecological centre.

The features characteristic of the ecological margins are the preponderance of wild animals and plants, sparse human population, unproductive soil for agriculture, lack of regular water supply, and only very limited internal communication, making the area virtually inaccessible. The distinctive features of the ecological centre are the presence of domesticated animals and plants, availability of soil productive for cultivation, perennial source of water, dense human population, and a network of paths and roads for internal communication.

In ecological features they are exclusive but interdependent. The various products of the ecological margins—for example, tools, implements, fruits, and beverages—supplement significantly the needs of people in the ecological centre. The resources of the ecological centre, for example, staple food crops, animal products, provide basic requisites for the people in the ecological margins. However, it remains to be seen how internal variation in the ecological pattern of the hinterland supports specialized tribal groups, and how interaction between margins and centre is realized through the common institution of the intertribal market.

CHAPTER IV

ETHNIC COMPONENTS OF THE BANARI REGION

I

THE Banari intertribal market serves over 20,000 persons drawn from 68 villages of the hinterland. Mapping the distribution of the population and the villages on the basis of the ecological divisions of the region suggested in the previous chapter, some 4,500 persons are found in the ecological margins and some 16,000 live in the ecological centre of the hinterland. This ratio is almost inversely related to the geographical area occupied by the ecological margins and centre of the hinterland. Likewise out of 68 villages, 14 are located on the margins and 54 are within the centre. Although exact statistics on the dispersion of population in the region are not available, the distribution of the villages indicates that as we proceed from the valley to the hills and plateaus the density decreases. Culturally, the valley contains technologically more advanced tribal communities than those who inhabit the hills and plateaus. In the valley there are nucleated villages of agricultural Oraon, Munda, and Hindu, together with partly agricultural communities of Lohra blacksmiths, Kumhar potters, Chik-Baraik weavers, and Bania traders. The hills and plateaus are occupied by dispersed villages of the horticultural Birjia, Khaira, Kisan, and the ironsmelting Asur, the semi-nomadic Birhor food gatherers, rope-makers, and hunters, as well as the Turi and Māhli basket-makers. The distribution of these communities suggests close correlation between ecological and cultural patterns in the region. The least favourable areas, the ecological margins, are settled by horticultural, artisan, food gathering, and hunting communities, while the most favourable area of the region, the ecological centre, is occupied by agricultural and partly agricultural communities.

Some cultural expressions in the region are based on ecological differences; for example, the natives' conception of direction does not reflect our east-west and north-south axis, but altitude, "higher" or "lower." The villages on hills and plateaus are referred to as "higher," while the villages in the valley are referred to as "lower." Even in a village one hears people distinguishing between two hamlets as higher and lower, the hamlet high up and the hamlet down below.

Apart from socio-economic differences between peoples in the hills and plateaus, and those in the valley, one finds evidence of status differences expressed in terms of "hill-billies" and "valley-dwellers". There is conspicuous difference between the dress of the people on the margins and that of those in the centre. Settlers of the hills are generally ill-clad, the men wearing a loin-cloth and the women with short skirts and bare body. The dress of the people of the valley is more elaborate than that of the hill-settlers. Intertribal contacts are more frequent among the people of the valley than between those who live on the hills and plateaus. The latter are relatively isolated and inaccessible while the former, through a network of paths and roads, find contacts easy to achieve. Although natives of the region belong to three different linguistic groups, the Austro-Asiatic Munda, the Dravidian Oraon, and the Indo-European Sadan, there are conspicuous dialectical differences among the people who live in the hills and plateaus and those who live in the valley. In the hills and plateaus the dialect varies even among the Munda speaking tribes : the Asur speaks Asuri ; the Birhor, Birhori ; and the Munda, Mundari dialects. In the valley, although linguistic variation among the Dravidian Oraon and the Indo-European Hindu castes is present, the Hindi dialect, Sadani has come to be the *Lingua franca* of all the tribes and castes.

Administratively, the ecological margins of the hinterland have remained in the backwaters, receiving much less attention than the valleys. All the aforementioned differences, as well as the absence of intertribal markets in the hills and plateaus, lend stress to the cultural importance of the valley to the region. It would seem, therefore, that the two concepts of the cultural margins and the cultural centre may be vital in explaining cultural differences within a particular regional cultural pattern.

II. The Village as a Nucleus of Regional Culture

The people of the Banari region may be described as belonging to primitive or peasant culture, living in villages. The villages toward the cultural margins consist generally of dispersed homesteads, sometimes spreading over four miles. The villages near the cultural centre of the region are generally nucleated, or clustered. Most villages in the region, except those of the semi-nomadic Birhor and some sedentary tribes such as the horticultural Birjia, Kharia, and Asur—all of which are found in the cultural margins—include members of two or more tribal and/or caste communities. It has also been observed that the number of tribes living in one village declines as one moves from the areal or ecological centre to the margins; villages become smaller and more dispersed; the population becomes scattered. In the valley, one finds villages consisting of tribal elements and castes, but on the hills and plateaus such villages are few, although some include more than one tribe.

The geography and history of the region provide some explanations of the distribution of human population in the margins and the centre.

The primitive occupational bases of tribal groups on the ecological margins require a large area for supporting even smaller groups; hence, large nucleated villages are unknown. The iron-smelting Asurs depend on large tracts of woods and hills for extracting fuel and iron ores with their limited indigenous technology. The horticultural Birjia and Kharia require large forests for their shifting cultivation; and the semi-nomadic Birhors need still wider areas because the creepers from which they make ropes and the supply of monkeys to be trapped soon become scarce in any one area. The economic base of the tribes and the castes living in the valley is agricultural. Agricultural lands and fertile soil are available only in the valley. Perhaps this fact has been largely responsible for nucleated villages in the valley, and also the absence of such villages on hills and plateaus.

The history of Chota Nagpur, recorded very ably by Roy (1915), throws further light on the distribution of tribal communities in this area. The original settlers of the region were the Austro-Asiatic Munda and their cognates, namely, Asur,

Birjia, Birhor, and several other communities of doubtful affinity, such as Chik-Baraik, Māhli, and Turi. Some still speak an Austric dialect. Even today some communities of Munda are to be found in the ecological margins of the region, although the majority are concentrated in other areas of Chota Nagpur. Historical evidence shows that the Munda were driven to the interior of the region by the Dravidian Oraon, who arrived later from the north via the North Koel River Valley (Birt 1913). The isolation of the Munda in the regional margins helped them to develop a symbolic relationship with their environment and to develop special occupations. The Asur smelted iron and supplied iron tools to the rest of the region ; the Birhor made ropes which were required by other tribes and castes ; the horticultural tribes supplied maize and millet to the peoples of the region ; the Māhli and Turi manufactured baskets and combs for them and played drums and pipes at tribal, village, or regional festivals ; the agricultural tribes, Oraon and others, provided cereal and staple foods to the peoples. The very specialization of these tribal communities created a need for interdependence among themselves which was, as we shall see, realized through the institution of the intertribal market.

The Oraons, who are numerically the largest tribe in the region, forming 68 per cent of the total regional population, constitute the dominant community in the valley. Although we do not have evidence for the exact date of immigration to the region—which occurred sometime in the first millennium B.C. (Dalton 1872 : 167)—we are told by Oraon folklore that they drove out most of the original valley settlers, established valleys, occupied fertile lands, and practised agriculture. They also made a treaty with the earlier landowners which allowed some to remain as settlers in the valley (Roy 1915 : 39).

Six per cent of the regional population in 1959 belonged to Hindu castes. There is no written evidence of Hindu migration into the region. Roy (1915 : 42) tells us of frequent inroads of Hindus during the seventeenth and eighteenth centuries A.D., who plundered the area but returned to their country. The local folklore still retains accounts of these events. Presently, the Hindu castes are not concentrated in any part of the region ; they are distributed in groups of five-to-ten families in villages of the valley. The Hindu population, except a few families of Rajput landlords, belong to the lower stratum of the Hindu caste system. There are the Ahir cattle herders, the Hazam barbers, the Kumhar potters, the Chamar cobblers, the Lohra ironsmiths, and the Bania traders.

III

From what we have seen above, the cultural setting of the Banari region reveals considerable complexity : there are over twenty tribal and caste groups, or communities, ranging from food gatherers, shifting cultivators, and artisans to agriculturalists ; such communities live in settlements ranging from dispersed to highly nucleated villages. In this diversity of types of residence, there is at least one meaningful basis of classification : those who live in villages inhabited by people belonging to only one tribe, and those who live in mixed villages of tribes and castes. The former type is met in the hills and plateaus, the cultural margins, while the latter is found in the valleys.

Culturally, both types of village communities bear close resemblance to Redfield's (1960) primitive culture and folk, or peasant culture respectively. It should, however, be pointed out that the cultural centre of the Banari region includes peasant culture inasmuch as it has more peasant characteristics than the cultural margins. The cultural margins reveal primarily primitive culture inasmuch as they possess more characteristics definitive of Redfield's "little community" than of his peasant community. In other words, the above characterization reflects relative positions rather than absolutes. Let us now examine some cultural characteristics of the margins and the centre of the region.

The Cultural Margins : The "Little Community" : Primitive Culture

Dispersed villages on the cultural margins of Banari are occupied by horticultural Birjia and Kharia, and the food gatherers, rope-makers and hunter Birhor. Culturally, they represent a single, composite type, which may be called "primitive," or "little community." These villages are relatively isolated, being located in the inaccessible hills and plateaus. They are small, the population of any one village ranging from 28 to 100 persons. Individually distinctive and yet homogeneous, they are amenable to holistic observation. Most villages in the cultural margins are occupied by a single tribal group, but a few are occupied by more than one. Nonetheless, they can be said to belong to a type called a "little community" (Redfield 1960 : 4).

In a classic little community, the above characteristics are supplemented by such traits as the all-providing self-sufficiency of the community. Self-sufficiency is a seasonal characteristic of the communities living in the margins of the Banari region. For example, the Birhors who depend on food gathering, collecting, and hunting, are basically a self-sufficient group during the monsoon, when they are cut off from outside contacts. However, in the remaining part of the year they produce surplus commodities like ropes, monkey hides, and honey, which they exchange for staple grains and other items from neighbouring communities at the intertribal market. Likewise, the horticultural Kharia, Birjia, and Asur remain isolated and self-sufficient during the monsoon, but interact with outside communities in other seasons.

Whether tribal communities in the cultural margins of the Banari region belong to an ideal primitive type or not is perhaps open to question, but the fact that they differ significantly in cultural characteristics from the peasant communities of the cultural centre of the region is readily apparent.

The Cultural Centre : Mixed Village : Peasant Culture

In the cultural centre there are 54 mixed villages, each of which has four to ten endogamous tribal or caste groups represented in its populace. The village of Banari exemplifies the kind of mixed village, found in the cultural centre.

The nucleated settlement of Banari, according to census in 1959, is peopled by 478 persons belonging to eight different tribal and caste groups. Of these, the Oraon and the Hindu landlord Rajput, both agriculturists, constitute 67.8 per cent and 1.2 per cent respectively. The Māhli and the Turi, partly agriculturists and basket-makers, 8 per cent and 5.2 per cent respectively; the Chik-Baraik weavers, 7.8 per cent; the Lohra blacksmiths, 4.3 per cent; the Kumhar potters, 8 per cent; and the Bania traders, 3.7 per cent. Agriculture is the basic source of livelihood of all groups represented in the village; even people who are artisans find a basic security in pursuing some agricultural activities. The tribal and caste groups of Banari, in spite of their separate traditions, reinforced by the practice of endogamy, share with each other some basic peasant characteristics. Depending solely or partly upon agriculture for subsistence, the villagers are in intimate association with the land. In Banari, land is conceived as one's prized possession, and one repeatedly hears the natives saying, "As long as you have a piece of land, you will not starve". Agricultural work in the village is considered the best occupation; even the Bania traders, who make most of their money by trade, own and farm land because to do so carries prestige.

The village of Banari is a unit; its people, tribe, and castes, even though of different origins, are interdependent, a fact emphasized by their socio-economic specialization (Sinha 1961). They share common environmental problems, common problems of agriculture, and belong to the same administrative unit, and above all, they exhibit allegiance to the Sarna, a sacred grove which is a sacred symbol of the village deity. Each tribal and caste group in the village has a network of horizontal ties with members of its own group in different villages of the region and even beyond. Social, religious, and political ties with people and places outside the village make the villagers of Banari a part of a larger social system, a characteristic so important in a peasant society. By producing surplus staple crops in the region, the people of Banari extend their economic ties to people of other areas. They become a part of the wider economic institution—the market system—which in turn influences their economic behaviour. The location of the intertribal market at Banari accelerates this process.

The people of the village of Banari have preserved their tradition through folk literature, but there has been increasing influence from literate Hindu tradition because of the presence of the Hindu Literate caste of Rajput. Of late in Banari, there has been established a formal school, a post office, agencies of state welfare, community development, and forest range, all of which expose community members to the world beyond their own village and the region. A Hindu Rajput family subscribes to a daily newspaper. The presence of a Hindu temple in the village makes it a part, however infinitesimal, of a tradition which extends far beyond the village, the cultural centre, and the cultural region of the Banạri. Banari may thus be considered a peasant village, and the people of Banari, therefore, participate in peasant culture; inasmuch as Banari is representative of the mixed villages of the regional centre, the cultural centre may also be properly characterized as having a peasant culture.

CHAPTER V

THE BANARI INTERTRIBAL MARKET

I

THE Banari intertribal market is located on the eastern bank of the North Koel River in the centre of the Banari region. It is connected to the settlements of the region by an intricate network of unsurfaced roads and bridle and foot-paths; some of these serve the market and the people throughout the year, but others become impassable during the monsoon. However, a hard-surfaced road, terminating at Banari, connects the area with the outside world at Lohardaga, the nearest town and railroad terminus, forty miles to the south-east, and, in turn, with district headquarters at Ranchi, eighty-two miles in the same direction.

There is no written record covering the origin and growth of the Banari market. On the basis of folk history and a few documents, however, it is possible to reconstruct three historical phases of its development. In the first, it was a centre of activities for the indigenous communities of the hinterland. In the second, it was augmented by settlements of immigrant Hindu peasants, potters, and traders. The third, or contemporary, phase is characterized by progressive adaptation to ever-increasing external influences.

Indigenous legends and folk tales refer to Banari as one of the oldest markets in Chota Nagpur. The traditional history of the Oraon migration contains reference to the Koel River and apparently also to Banari as the place whence the Oraon dispersed to the Chota Nagpur plateaus. Oraon folk tales refer to times when a visit to the market through dense forest and country infested with wild animals required two days. "In those days," runs an Oraon account, "the market was the place where festivals were held, large gatherings were seen, kinsmen were met, conflicts were resolved, marriages were negotiated, and brides were handed over to grooms." The commodities entering the market were few. The Oraon and Birjia brought rice, corn, and cotton; the Birhor brought ropes, honey, and monkey hides; the Asur, their indigenous iron implements; the Chik-Baraik, handwoven cloths. These commodities were exchanged at the market through direct barter. A Chik-Baraik would exchange a pair of loin-cloths for two basketfuls of corn or one basketful of rice from an Oraon or a Birjia, for one monkey hide or four pairs of ropes from a Birhor. However, an Asur with an iron plough could not barter it directly for loin-cloths with a Chik-Baraik. The Asur might barter his plough to an Oraon for rice and then transfer this to the Chik-Baraik in exchange for cloths. The oral literature contains no reference to the use of any "general purpose money" or "special purpose money" (Bohannan 1959 : 502).

The Banari market entered another phase when immigrant Hindus began to settle in the hinterland during the nineteenth century (Roy 1915 : 51). Some were agriculturists, and others were only part-time agricultural specialists, also working as potters, ironsmiths, and traders. To these economically specialized groups, the market provided a ready-made institution for trading their commodities, and in time they established interdependent relationships with the indigenous communities. According to tradition, as reported by a Hindu settler, "Our forefathers came to the area, reclaimed land for livelihood, made friends with the natives, learned their languages, and adopted their system of economy, and in the course of time included some native gods and spirits in their pantheon."

Stories relate how money introduced by the Hindus soon disappeared among the natives who used the coins for necklaces and ornaments rather than as a medium of exchange. The natives, in short, treated money as a commodity, and the Hindus, in turn, adopted the native system of barter at the market. The appearance of a specialized group of Hindu traders, however, altered the situation. Although there was still no commerce with the outside world, the sedentary traders made a living by redistributing the commodities of the hinterland at the market and providing an alternative to the earlier pattern of sequential bartering. An Asur, for example, who wanted to exchange his iron hoe for a pair of loin-cloths from a Chik-Baraik weaver, but was unable to make a direct barter, could now do so through the mediation of a Hindu trader, serving as a middleman.

The market continued to serve as a multi-purpose institution. People from the hinterland visited it as a matter of routine; they transferred, bartered, or exchanged commodities; they met kinsmen, friends and acquaintances and thus reinforced their social contacts; they arranged marriages and extended invitations; they made decisions regarding collective activities and festivals in the communities of the hinterland; they negotiated conflicts and disputes; and they engaged in various recreational activities. In the absence of more modern means, the tribal market served as the only source of mass communication in the hinterland.

The third, or contemporary, phase in the history of the Banari market began around the middle of the present century, when the national government initiated a new welfare project for the hill tribes. In 1950 Banari was reached by a hard-surfaced road, which was soon plied by trucks and buses. Itinerant traders entered the market with a wide variety of new commodities, ranging from stick matches to modern agricultural implements. The road brought government agents, school teachers, social reformers, forest contractors, political leaders, tourists, and other alien Hindus into contact with the hinterland. The market served as the point of entry for all these people and became a centre of contacts between the hill tribes and the Hindus, between peoples speaking different languages and having different customs, values, and world views, and between these who still practised a barter economy and those who lived by a "modern self-regulating market economy."

The following excerpt from an interview with a seventy-eight-year-old Hindu trader whose grandfather settled in this region, provides some light on the character and composition of the intertribal market in the past:

> . . . I have been coming to this market for generations, since the time of my grandfather, for over sixty years now. But I do not know about the origin of this market; it is so very old. It existed during the Sepoy Mutiny (1857) and it must have been there before.
>
> When I was a boy, these tribal people did not know how

to put on clothes. The Oraon, Munda, and others in the valley used to put on a small loin-cloth like you see the natives of the hills wearing now at the market. They did not know how to burgain price; whatever we gave them in exchange for their commodities they gladly accepted. My father used to buy grains, maize, rice, from the natives. He would sometimes give them a ten-rupee bill, but they would not accept it. They were glad to have a handful of pennies instead. The shops at the market were mainly of regional commodities: rice, paddy, maize, millet and some vegetables, native spices, oil, salt, baskets, flutes, drums, pottery, ropes, chickens, meat, etc. One or two shops of nickel, silver, and brass ornaments, and beads, were enough. The native weavers sold handloomed clothes; none cared for mill-made clothes; only a few like us [Hindu settlers] used mill-made clothes. We introduced mill-made clothes and ready-made garments into the market after the Second World War. It was then that this road was paved, and the natives saw many outsiders. There were only a few permanent huts at the market place. All these [pointing to the huts] were built by us, the Hindu traders. Not many urban traders from Lohardaga or elsewhere attended the market every week. We went to towns, once a month to Lohardaga, once in several months to Ranchi, to sell the commodities purchased from the natives and to buy goods that we sold at the market. Our forefathers, like those of other professional traders in this market, had settled in the valley. They kept in touch with towns and the relatives outside. The problem of communication was acute. There was no all-weather road. We were practically isolated during the monsoon when rivers and streams overflowed. Most of the time we carried loads on the backs of bullocks and ponies. Bullock carts were almost unknown. There was no permanent habitation near the market place. The Banari village was one furlong away, separated by trees and bushes. Sometimes leopards used to carry off ponies or bullocks from the market place in the evenings. We had to keep our bullocks inside and guarded with fire around [them].

Things have changed now. My grandfather used to say that in his time market was held by sunrise and everything was over by noon. The natives travelled to the market in large groups, sometimes leaving their villages by midnight, using torchlight to cross the wild country . . .

I was told during the old days this place [the area covered by the market place] was owned by nobody. It belonged to everyone in the region . . . it was communal property and they [his forefathers] said it was the safest place in the region. Everyone, friend or foe, attended the market with security; nobody could even take revenge of his feuds with others at the market place. There was no law, but they said it was a custom. However, after we [Hindus] settled in the region, the zamindar [landlord] owned the market site. He had supposedly received a deed from the British Raj [government]. He collected revenues from the traders and the native settlers in cash or kind and, perhaps, paid a portion of it to the British Raj. It is only since this Congress Raj [present Indian national government] was formed that they auctioned stalls at the markets. Last year the B.D.O. (Block Development and Revenue Officer) auctioned the stalls in this market and there were six bidders. This contractor [pointing to the agent who collected tolls] made the highest bid. He accepts only cash as the toll, even from the native sellers. He is unscrupulous. Although the government has fixed toll rates for selling different commodities, this contractor always makes excuses for charging exorbitant rates. He cannot displace us [meaning those who have permanent huts at the market place], but he can certainly demand high prices, even a hundred rupees . . . from anyone who wants to build a shed at the market place.

II

The Banari intertribal market, which is held on Mondays, has occupied the same site for several generations. The nucleus, or the centre, of the market place constitutes an area of five acres, but the area of its periphery, or maximum extension, varies from one market day to another. In the course of the present study, the total area occupied by people attending the market varied from five to twenty-five acres during different seasons.

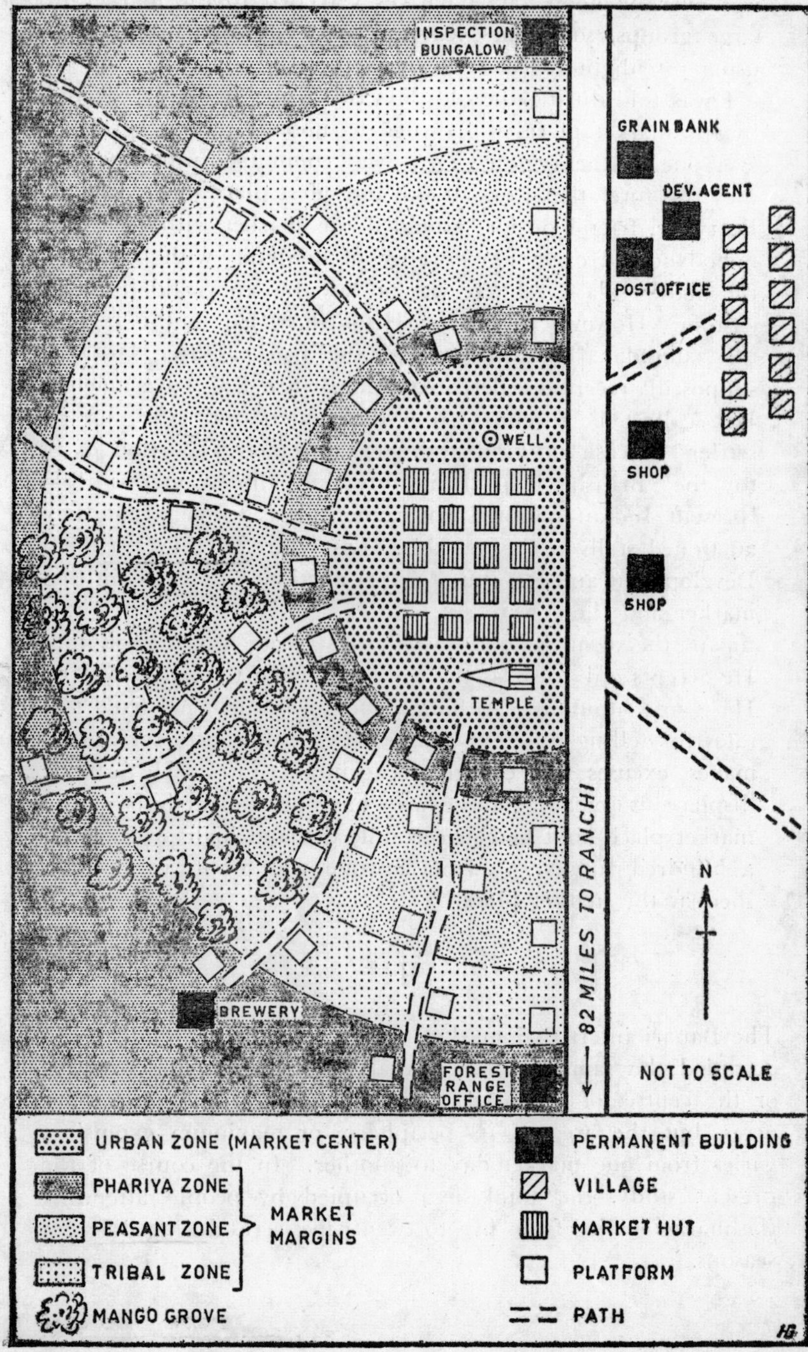

Sketch map of the Banari Market place.

A quick look at the map of the market place provides a broad idea of its orientation, size, and composition (see Map IV). The northern part of the market place covers the open non-cultivated land ; the southern boundary is marked by the forest range office ; the eastern boundary fronts on the surfaced road ; and the western boundary covers a large mango grove. During recent years permanent habitations have appeared in the peripheries of the market place. Across the highway, where is located a stop for the commercial buses running twice every day and thrice on market days, two permanent shops have appeared ; these serve refreshments and tea to the passengers. The Hindu traders who operate these shops have also built their houses alongside them. Two hundred yards west of the market place is located a small brewery, run by an urban trader, which does a thriving business on market days. In the north, across the field, have appeared, during the last five years, a post office, the office of a community development agent, and a grain bank of the State Welfare Department. Close by is a bungalow of the State Highway Department where travelling government officials spend nights, and urban visitors, tourists, adventurers, or anthropologists, can stay for small payments. The nucleated village of Banari is fifty yards north-east of the market place.

A close scrutiny of the layout of the site of the Banari intertribal market reveals two broad zones : one, the large expanse of land surrounding the cluster of huts, where one finds natural shade of trees and orchards, and the other, an area at the centre where one finds huts laid out in five more or less parallel rows.

The first zone is occupied by tribes and castes of the hinterland. This zone may be called the native zone, or the market margins.

The second zone, surrounded by the first, is occupied by urban traders and such functionaries as the landlords, contractors, police, revenue officers, tribal welfare and forest range officials, community development agents, and postman, who all have continuous contacts with the urban centres of Chota Nagpur. This zone may be called the urban zone, the market centre of the intertribal market.

If we examine closely the spatial distribution of the tribal and caste groups in the market margins, we find an interesting concentric pattern. The area on the periphery of the market margins is occupied by the Phariyas, the natives who play the role of socio-economic mediator between the urban and the native peoples. Next, the area running parallel to the Phariya zone is occupied by the artisan tribes from the hills and plateaus of the hinterland, which is in turn followed by the zone occupied by the peasants and partly artisan communities of the valley. Inside the peasant zone and almost parallel to it is the area occupied by the Phariyas, a zone characterizing transition from the market margins to the market centre. The innermost zone of the market place, the market centre, is occupied by the urban traders, administrative agents, and other peoples constantly in touch with neighbouring urban centres of Chota Nagpur.

The spatial distribution of available commodities also followed the above concentric pattern as one might expect. At the market margins, in the marginal zone, we find products of the hills and forests; in the artisan zone we find commodities manufactured by artisan peoples of the hinterland; in the peasant zone agricultural commodities; and at the market centre, in the urban zone we find urban commodities.

As we will see later, this arrangement of peoples and products at the market place reflects not only the socio-economic pattern of the region but also the process by which urban influences bring about cultural changes in the region.

III

The Banari intertribal market operates, as mentioned, once a week, on Mondays. For the rest of the week the market place remains deserted. Cattle, goats, and other animals roam at will; in summer they also use the open huts as a shelter from the scorching sun. Teen-age boys and girls who graze the cattle find these huts a convenient place to relax and rest. Children from the neighbouring settlement of Banari sometimes use the market place for sports and games. Pedestrians also find the market place a ready-made place to rest in the shade.

As the Banari intertribal market operates only on Mondays, the natives of the region customarily associate Mondays with

Banari and Banari with Mondays. In fact, the alternate name of Banari is Sombar Bazar, which means "Monday market." In order to better understand how the intertribal market functions, it may be appropriate to quote here from the author's observations and notes on the Banari intertribal market relevant to one market day in the winter of 1959.

It was observed yesterday (Sunday) morning that the huts at the market place were cleaned, and coated with cowdung paste. There were eight women from the Banari village; each one repaired five to nine sheds during the forenoon. On being asked, the women said that each had a contract with the traders who owned the huts. They received 25 Naye Paise [about 5 cents] for each hut cleaned. Besides cleaning some huts, they also patched up holes and repaired broken floors. They swept the open space around the huts. Close to the market centre, a native was erecting a platform, 5′ × 3′ × 1′, for a Phariya. By 2 P.M., the women had finished their work, and the centre of the market place was neat and clean. Although nobody stayed to guard against any tampering by children or animals, surprisingly enough nobody interfered with the huts.

At 5-20 P.M. the Ranchi-Netarhat bus arrived. Seven sacks were unloaded. Each belonged to an urban trader from Lohardaga.

Soon after the bus left, the women who had been working in the huts earlier appeared at the market place. They had wood fuel in their hands, which they distributed in different huts. They also made a small hearth in each hut, drew water from the neighbouring wells, and stored it in one or two pitchers in each hut.

Another bus from Lohardaga arrived at 7 P.M. The passengers—most of them urban traders—were packed like gunnybags inside the bus. Their goods were stored on top of the bus in sacks and boxes. One told me that they were coming from Adar, where an intertribal market is held on Sundays. Some had brought with them only a part of their trade goods; the rest they had loaded on a bullock cart which would arrive the following morning. Alighting from the bus, each settled in his hut, stored his belongings, cooked meal, ate, and slept therein. Until 9 P.M., one could see smoke radiating from the market place, and hear quiet conversations and joking among the traders and the natives of the Banari village.

This morning (Monday) brought life to the market centre. The huts which remained desolated on week-days now had urban traders staying in them. There were forty-one persons in all, occupying as many huts. Soon after dawn, the native women appointed to clean the huts came in, washed the utensils, cleaned the hearths, and arranged for cooking the morning meal. Meanwhile bullock carts carrying goods of the urban traders from other intertribal markets began arriving. They were unloaded into various huts at the market centre. Later I observed four Oraon women engaged in cleaning the open booths of the Phariyas near the market centre. They were cleaning them in extreme haste. Some men from the Banari village came to assist the women. They drew water from the well and stored it in pitchers in various huts. All this was done by 9 P.M., and the traders finished the morning meal, cleaned their huts, and began laying their wares. At half past nine I made a round of the market place.

There were sixty-three huts at the market centre; fifty-nine of them were occupied by urban traders who had their commodities displayed. Twenty-four were shops for groceries like salt, sugar, spices, flour, pulse, mustard oil, kerosene oil and tobacco. Nine dealt with mill-made clothes; nine displayed dime-store goods, like mirrors, combs, nail polish, ribbons, notebooks, purses, belts, pens, and pencils. Eight showed various kinds of sweets and candies. Five offered tailored garments; two displayed various kinds of silver, brass, nickel, and bead ornaments; and two shops were selling brass cooking utensils. There were one, two, or more persons in each shop; most were urban traders, but some traders had local assistants. Four huts were unoccupied; I was told they belonged to the Hindu landlord, two to Hindu traders, and one to the tax collector of the market, respectively. The latter's shed was also used by government agents, the postman, police, land revenue clerk, forester, community development agent, and others.

At half past nine the market centre was humming, but it

was not because of the tribal or caste people from the region, but because of people from outside the region, itinerant traders, whose practice was to move from one weekly market to another and then return to their urban home for a day or two every week. I was told that some had ties in several regions of Chota Nagpur, and I felt that by recurring visits alone they would have established a network of relationship with peasant and tribal communities of the region. At places where I stopped for a while and listened to conversations of traders, I found that they were talking about a multitude of things, ranging from Prime Minister Nehru's policy on the Indo-Tibet border to common jokes of the hill-billies of the region. It was obvious that the traders did not engage in economic activities alone; they carried their traditions and values into the regions visited, and, most probably, they carried away traditions of the regions.

By ten o'clock I saw some people from the valley coming to the market place. Two rode bicycles and nine came on foot, but each had one or two gunnybags and five to eight Pailas, metal or wooden containers used for measuring grains and other commodities. There were two Phariyas, natives working as socio-economic mediators, functioning somewhat like an exchange bank, for the natives and the urban traders. After arriving at the market centre, each went to his urban trader. I was told later that each urban trader, trading in groceries or textiles or grains, had appointed a number of Phariyas through whom he conducted business with the natives of the region. I also learned that some traders, whose interest was to purchase native produce, advanced and loaned money to the natives through the Phariyas, hoping to assure that the native's produce would be sold to the trader and to no one else. Later I observed that a Phariya received from his urban trader a certain amount of cash with which he was supposed to do the business of the day.

Gradually tribes and caste men from the region began coming in from every direction. By half past ten the market centre was in full swing; the margins, however, had only a few people. Some urban traders, perhaps recent additions to the group, were erecting cloth canopies close to the market centre. It was found that two of them carried tailored garments and mill-made clothes ; one of them traded dime-store goods ; two of them traded aluminium utensils, which were manufactured in South India but were imported here from Ranchi. One urban trader had a shop for rubber shoes and chappals made of rejected auto tires. Interviews revealed that these people had been making weekly visits to this market for the last five years. It appeared that these traders, although providing novel commodities to the peoples of the region, were like urban traders who had occupied the nucleus of the market centre. When I asked one of them why he had not built a hut like other urban traders at the market centre, he replied, "I am new to this market ; I have been coming here for only the last three and a half years, but they have been visiting for generations. . ."

It was quarter to eleven. One could see still more people coming to the market place in small and large groups from every direction. One group of natives were the Hindu potters ; each was carrying a dozen or so earthenware pots and vessels on his head, arranged and tied intricately. I counted one group of six persons and others of four, five, three, and three : in all, twenty-one persons were carrying pots and pitchers. They went to the eastern side of the market place and settled in the margins. It appeared that each one knew where to spread his wares. Another set of people arrived at about the same time, also in small groups. They were the basket-makers, Turi and Māhli. Thirty-nine of them occupied the south-east corner of the market margins. Each had varieties of commodities, such as baskets, oval boxes, winnowing fans, and containers, all made of bamboo. The Māhli also displayed combs, flutes, pipes, and drums. In fact, when the Māhli were coming to the market, they were beating and playing drums. Gradually the native weavers, Chik-Baraik, appeared at the market place and occupied seats at the margins. They displayed their handloom clothes on the grass. There were twenty-one of them by midday. On the western margins nine native barbers had occupied one row ; they were already busy cropping the hair of the natives.

At the market centre, rather close to the highway, I was introduced to a contractor who collected taxes weekly from urban traders and folk sellers at the market place. This middle-aged man had arrived on a bicycle from fourteen miles away, outside the region. He was a Hindu, literate, and was working as an agent for the person who had purchased from the Revenue Department of the State Government the right to collect taxes. He had a notebook in hand, and, assisted by two native Oraons, he made a round of the market centre and margins, enumerating different kinds of shops.

At twelve past ten a truck stopped on the highway. Three persons alighted from the front seats. (I could not count the number of people standing in the rear of the truck; there must have been about twenty.) I learned later that one of the three was a forest contractor and another, a forest ranger; the third was the driver, and the tribesmen in the rear, forest labourers. The forest contractor took a seat in an open shed, pulled out a long notebook and spread out different denominations of coins and bills near him. Then the labourers who had worked for him during the past week stepped in to collect their wages. He paid wages to seventy-eight persons. The forest ranger sat in another corner. Some tribesmen—Oraon, Kisan, Birjia, and Māhli—came to him for permits to pick up trees in the forest. Some asked him when a work order for cutting the coops was to be issued and wanted to know how many labourers would be required.

The tribal and caste peoples from valley and hills who had been pouring into the market all this time radiated to different parts of the market place. Most had carried with them some commodity for barter, exchange, or sale. I could see that some were carrying rice, puffed rice, paddy, corn, vegetables, or chickens. The men carried commodities in gunnybags or small sacks, on Bahngi, a kind of native balance for carrying heavy loads. The women carried things in baskets on their heads. The children accompanying them also had some bottles or bags to carry. It was obvious that they had put on neat dresses for the occasion; young boys and girls were especially conspicuous (I say this because I have seen them in their daily clothing in the villages). Some natives carried drums and flutes which they played at intervals on their way to the market.

As the people came near the market place they confronted

the Phariyas who had taken their seats at almost all the points of entry to the market margins and the market centre. The Phariyas were also spread out on the roads and foot-paths converging at the market. They had occupied all strategic positions. I suspect that if I had plotted the exact spatial distribution of the Phariyas, I would have ended up with at least two rings : one connecting the end points of the market margins and another in between the market centre and the market margins. The primary business of the Phariyas was to attract the tribesmen so that they might sell their commodities to them. They did this by calling loudly to the natives who passed by. Some persons were attracted by the call and went to the first Phariya they met, some to the second, and some moved ahead by ignoring them all until they reached Phariyas near the market centre. It was interesting to observe that some tribesmen by-passed the paths and entered the market margins through open fields. They, however, went straight to the Phariya or the urban trader of their choice. One said that he was going to his own Phariya, and he by-passed the path because he did not want to be bothered by other Phariyas. Others said that they wanted to sell their commodities by themselves. Still others replied that they had commodities—such as fried rice and vegetables—which could only be bartered. While making a round of the booths of the Phariyas, I noticed that most had collected only four kinds of commodities, namely, rice-paddy, corn, lac or mahua, a kind of wild flower used for making beer. They were buying these commodities for cash from these natives, and measuring them with the Pailas, the native measuring cups which calculated the volume rather than weight of a commodity. The Phariya would say to the natives, "Chabal char Paila" (four pailas rice for one rupee), "Dhan sat Paila" (seven pailas of paddy for one rupee), and so forth. Some persons, I observed, questioned the real volume of the Paila used by the Phariyas. They wanted to verify the Phariya's Paila with their own which they carried. When they were satisfied, they gave their commodity, collected cash, and moved to the market centre for purchasing urban commodities which they could not have purchased without cash.

It was a quarter past one when I picked up conversation with one of the natives, Mangra Oraon ; he was carrying two bags of rice. His wife had a basket on her head in which, I later found, there were thirteen eggs, about two dozen egg-plants, about two pounds of green peppers, and a bagful of native pills used for fermenting liquor. She had made pills by grinding the bark of a wild tree. Besides his wife, there were Mangra's two teen-aged sons ; one had a flute in his hand, and the other was carrying two empty bottles. Although these persons were identified by Mangra as the only persons who came with him, I had observed only a short time before that they were part of a larger group of eighteen persons who entered the market, together. When I probed further, Mangra told me that they were his co-villagers. Mangra was talking to his Phariya and asked the rate of exchange for rice and unloaded his bags. Mangra did not examine the Paila used by the Phariya. The Phariya measured rice and gave him seven rupees and fifty paise. There was little conversation between Mangra and this Phariya. While walking with me, Mangra told me that he had known the Phariya for a very long time. As we approached the market centre, Mangra's wife walked over the margins, without speaking a word to her husband or to her sons. I followed Mangra and his sons, who went to the market centre, first to a grocery shop. There he greeted the trader (it seemed they knew each other well), asked for a bottle of kerosene oil, a bottle of mustard oil, one large dry tobacco leaf, two pounds of salt, and a pound of brown sugar. Mangra kept all these in his bag and took the two bottles from his son to carry himself. After paying the trader in cash, Mangra moved toward a shop of tailored garments. Stepping forward, he met several friends and acquaintances and, perhaps telling them that he would see them in the margins, went ahead to the store of tailored garments. There he purchased two bush-shirts for his sons. Both boys put on their shirts immediately. Mangra later gave ten Paise to each boy. Leaving them to take care of themselves, he went around the market place, meeting relatives, friends, and acquaintances from the region. Mangra's wife meanwhile had occupied a place in the market margins where agriculturist tribes and caste men bartered and sold their goods themselves. There were several rows of men and women selling fried rice, vegetables, chickens, eggs, puffed rice, parched rice, and various other native snacks and sweets. Mangra's wife was sitting on the row occupied by people from her village. She had placed her eggs in one corner, vegetables in another, fermenting pills in the third corner, and peppers in the fourth.

The Banari intertribal market was at its peak by 2 P.M. The market centre was overcrowded, and the market margins were flooded with people. A modest estimate would be something like three thousand people. Proceeding southward to the market margins, I noticed that the Birhor men were squatting in one area, spreading their ropes, monkey hides, and wooden vessels in rows. Their women were sitting nearby, having conversations with their relatives from other regional bands. I was told that some had gone to the market centre to purchase salt, oil, rice, and so forth. Later I noticed that a young Birhor had purchased a woollen scarf, another had purchased a tailored banian; a young girl had purchased a mirror and a comb. Another girl who had a new scarf said that it was a present from her fiancee.

Next to the Birhor, sitting almost at the southern end of the market margins, were the Asurs, selling leaf mats, raincoats made of leaves, and leaf plates. Some men looked after sales, others sat around idly, and still others had gone to different parts of the market for other business. Likewise, the Lohra blacksmiths were sitting in a row displaying their implements, plough shoes, and nails, along with their repair kits. Moving around the margins, I noticed three natives butchering goats and pigs and selling them by the piece for cash or commodities. In another part of the margins natives were selling fish.

Back in the market centre, I could see dozens of young boys and girls loitering around the shops which displayed novelties. A dozen boys and girls had crowded into a shop of dime-store goods. The two ornament shops were crowded with young girls who were examining and perhaps buying ornaments. Some girls standing by were commenting on the new jewellery designs. The huts of the urban grocers were overcrowded with men. I stepped into one hut and noticed that the trader was explaining to a Birjia how much he owed him. The trader had a notebook and a Hindu assistant who helped him in explaining accounts to his clients. Six other persons, two Oraons and four Asurs, were sitting in a corner awaiting their turns. I was told that this trader was also a moneylender. He advanced cash to tribesmen in times of scarcity or need, and collected it back with interest after they had harvested the crop. I moved to the other shops at the market centre. Everywhere, tribal people were settling their economic indebtedness to the urban moneylender. At one place I observed that an Oraon came to the urban trader before he had asked for anything; the trader asked how much he needed, and immediately gave an advance of five rupees.

In one hut the landlord of Banari was sitting on a chair. Six other natives were seated on a bench and a dozen others squatted on the floor. The landlord, who was also the head of the village Panchayat (council), was discussing individual and village problems with the tribesmen. When I stepped into his hut, he greeted me and offered me a vacant chair. I sat there for a while and listened to the conversations. A Munda sought advice, as to how he should deal with a revenue peon who had allegedly asked for a bribe to settle a dispute. Another person, Khaira Oraon, had received a summons from the court and wanted to know what he was supposed to do. Perhaps each one there had some kind of problem.

Next, I stopped at another hut where a community development worker was displaying new agricultural tools. He had collected a band of people from various villages, and he was explaining the advantages of the new implements. Close by, the local postman was delivering letters and money orders to persons who lived nine or ten miles away from the post office. A peon of the revenue office was issuing summons to tribesmen from different parts of the region. Close to the highway, near the market centre, I found a group of four persons surrounded by a large crowd; the four were singing songs accompanied by a harmonium, and at intervals, they were giving lectures (advertising) on the usefulness of

Burhiya-ka-kajal (eye-liner of the old lady), emphasizing especially its success in improving eyesight.

At quarter to four, I was back at the market margins. The Phariyas were almost at the end of their business of buying, but one could see tribal people coming back and forth to them. When I asked a Phariya why they grouped around him when they had nothing to sell, he replied, "They want to know what is happening around . . . in the region and outside."

Two small crowds were at the margins, one centred around a cockfight which was, I learned, the favourite recreation of the regional people at the market place. The two cocks belonged respectively to an Oraon from the valley and a Birjia from the hills. Another crowd was watching the tricks of a ten-year-old Māhli boy, who played music, danced, and sang with a cobra snake. Other small groups of people squatted near the brewery, drinking beer and discussing common issues. I was told that any customary problems, like kin conflicts, village feuds, marriage negotiations, violations of taboos, and so on, were discussed by the tribesmen only over beer-drinks.

Moving southward to the market margins, one could still see tribesmen bartering commodities. The Hindu potters had already sold about 80 per cent of their wares. When I asked one which community had purchased most of his wares, he replied, "Everyone, Oraon, Munda, Māhli, Baraik, Birhor, Asur, Birjia." The potter led me to believe that he knew how many pots he had to sell every week in this market. The Māhli and Turi had still some baskets left. Their clients also were from all the tribes and castes of the region. However, the Birhor had not been able to sell even 25 per cent of their ropes. As I talked to a Birhor chief, a tribal welfare agent of the State Government appeared on the scene and purchased all the ropes on behalf of the government; he paid twenty-five Paise for each rope. The ironsmith's repair business was still thriving; several Oraons from the valley were standing by to get their ploughknife sharpened. The Asurs had sold their mats, plates, and leaf raincoats. But still they sat around and discussed some problems. When I asked one Asur what was happening, he did not speak a word. However, a young Birjia told me later that a married woman from Dumbar Pat, an Asur village, had eloped with a man from Sakhoa Pani, another Asur village, on the ecological margins. The elderly Asurs from the region were trying to resolve the dispute between the two villages.

Some tribesmen selling at the market margins had not been able to dispose of even one-third of their commodities. One of the women had a basketful of guavas, a kind of local fruit; when I asked her why she did not sell them, she replied that nobody was willing to pay the price she wanted. Soon I discovered that this woman had decided to sell the fruits at her own price only; preferred to take them back home rather than sell them at a lower price. The theory of supply and demand did not make any difference to her; this was also true of other tribal sellers, as I found out.

The agriculturist tribesmen who sold grains themselves used Paila (containers) rather than a balance scale. Vegetables were sold according to the tribal principle of Kheja, arranging them in small bunches, each priced for cash or commodity.

It was five o'clock in the afternoon, and some people were on their way back home, but many were still squatting in groups near the market margins. At least a hundred groups remained scattered through the market. Each was socializing with relatives, friends, tribes and fellow caste men, and with other people from the region. Listening to the conversation of one group, I learned that they belonged to the same village. They were awaiting some of their co-villagers who had not yet finished their social business. A good many were carrying back salt, spices, oil, and tobacco. Some had purchased earthenwares; others, baskets, combs. clothes, garments, and the like. Boys and girls had purchased sweets, candies, and also novel toys. By 5 P.M. all members of the group were together, and soon they started for home.

At quarter past five I made a round of the booths of the Phariyas. Each booth was filled with maize, rice, lac, and mahua-flower. These were heaped separately on the floor. Some Phariyas had begun to weigh these commodities with the help of a balance scale. The urban traders who had advanced money to the Phariyas were supervising the weighing of commodities. They also helped in packing the commodities in gunnybags. When all the commodities had been weighed and sealed, the traders settled the rate, deducted the amount paid to the Phariya in the morning, and gave the balance to the Phariya. This was his wage for the day. By dusk most natives were on their way back home. The market margins were now quiet and clean.

In the market centre the landlord, contractor, forester, postman, community development agent, and other urban agents had already left for their respective residences. The traders were closing up their stalls. Some were calculating profit and loss, while others were busy in stock-taking of the day's transactions. One trader was talking about advancing potato seeds to the natives of the ecological margins for cultivation in the next monsoon. Another was discussing the excesses of the tax collector. They were also gossiping about tribal love-lores, someone saying, "How free these young men and women are ?" After dark, when the traders were cooking meal, relaxing and gossiping, I overheard someone ask about me, "Who was that young man ? Was he a government officer ? What was he observing so closely in our shops, and writing ?" "What was he doing, but surely a lot of different kinds of people you see now at the market," observed another.

I was told that they would be gone before dawn to some Tuesday market, or back to their urban homes, on bus, cycles, or bullock carts.

[The following morning] :

The market place was desolate ; not a single soul around!

IV. Seasonal Variation Of The Banari Intertribal Market

The foregoing dawn to dusk description of the Banari intertribal market, as recorded on a Monday in the winter of 1959, presents an ethnographic picture of the formation, function, and dispersion of the market components and brings out some observable differences between the market centre and the market margins. It also indicates the process of interactions among the urban, natives and the intervening Phariya zones, with the last serving as the area of socio-economic mediation, primarily between the other two.

Although the basic structure of the market remains the same on all Mondays throughout the year, there are still observable seasonal variations in the contents and components of the market. On a particular Monday, a political rally or election campaign may occur at the market place ; on another, one may find some reformist group organizing meetings there ; on still another, a government agent may be promoting public education, and so forth. But the functional role of these variables remains basically similar. The following Table provides an idea of the seasonal variation in the composition of the market.

TABLE 3

SEASONAL FLUCTUATIONS IN SPACE AND PARTICIPATION AT THE BANARI INTERTRIBAL MARKET
(Averages only)

	Area of the Market-place	*Number of Natives from the Hinterland*		*Urban Traders*
		Valley	*Hills and Plateaus*	
Winter (Nov.-Feb.)	21 acres	3,200	500	59
Summer (Mar.-June)	18 acres	2,900	400	47
Monsoon (July-Oct.)	3 acres	550	16	13

The above Table shows variation between three recognized seasons of the region. The winter, from November to March, marks the opening of activities in the ecological centre and the ecological margins of the region. The peasants in the valley harvest their crops ; the communities on hills and plateaus find their depleted natural resources restored after the rains ; tribal marriages are settled and celebrated in winter. Two important festivals of the region, Sohrai in November, and Fagua in February, are held in this season. These, besides many other factors, influence the tribal and caste people's interaction with the market, making it more frequent, intensive and significant,

During summer, March to June, in the valley some secondary crops, like pulse, wheat, and other grains are harvested, and the peasants bring them to the market. On the hills and plateaus, the people harvest maize and millet, and the forest resources remain available.

Although the tribesmen prepare themselves for combating the monsoon in this season, work and leisure are intermittent. Two important regional festivals, Sarhul and Karma, fall in this season and hence the market continues its boom and bloom although some decrease in activities is apparent.

Rains during the monsoon, July through October, make communication between the ecological centre and margins of the region difficult. Even in the valley the pace of movement slows down. The peasants prepare their fields; the artisans and the hill tribes find it difficult to secure raw materials from the forest. These affect the intertribal market.

The regional tribes and castemen correlate the importance of the market day with the size of its attendance. During the four regional festivals, one sees the largest aggregations at the market place. It is then that one finds the market functioning more as a cultural than as an economic institution. The rhythm of the seasons of the region is closely reflected in the rhythm of the market, so much so that a discriminating observer may tell you the season by looking at the market, and *vice versa*.

The Banari intertribal market mirrors the region it serves. The positions occupied in the hinterland by the tribal and caste groups are reflected in the manner in which they place themselves in the market. The intertribal market thus provides a basis for understanding and examining the regional ethnology.

The intertribal market also provides a common ground of interaction between the natives and the urbanites, and between the tribal and peasant, and the urban ways of life. In short, it is a centre of acculturation. The emergence of the native institution of Phariya, which we will examine at length in later chapters, demonstrates one of the more significant mechanisms by which acculturation operates in the intertribal market.

CHAPTER VI

ECONOMIC ROLE OF THE BANARI INTERTRIBAL MARKET

I

THE Banari intertribal market is the hub of economic life in the region. It serves as a centre of redistribution for resources and material goods of the occupationally diverse communities in the region, ranging from the Birhor food gatherers, rope-makers and hunters, to the Turi and Māhli basket-makers; the Asur iron smelters; the Birjia, Kharia, and Kisan horticulturalists; the Lohra blacksmiths; the Kumhar potters; the Chik-Baraik weavers; the Bania traders, and the Oraon, Munda and Hindu agriculturalists. The traditional role of the Banari intertribal market is thus one of maintaining internal economic balance and stability in the region. During recent years the intertribal market has played another role, for it has linked the native barter economy to the modern self-regulating market economy.

The traditional and the modern economic roles of the intertribal market are very clearly delineated at the market place. The economic transactions which take place at the margins of the market are of the traditional type, whereas the economic transactions which take place at the centre are concerned with the modern economic role of the market. Between the market margins and the centre, the Phariyas function, linking the traditional native economy to the modern self-regulating market economy.

Traditional economic transactions are carried on through barter; commodities are measured by volume rather than by weight; production is small in scale; concern is with consumer goods rather than trade goods; competition is absent, prices being fixed by traditionally determined relative values rather than as a result of the interplay of demand and supply of commodities.

The modern role of the market is characterized by the growing use of money, measurement by weight, the introduction of mass-produced and manufactured commodities, price fixing by demand and supply of commodities, and other typical characteristics of a self-regulating market economy.

II. Continuity of Native Economy

Two kinds of commodities enter the Banari intertribal market —general purpose commodities and special purpose commodities (Sinha 1963). General purpose commodities are of primary importance to the natives and are primarily produced inside the region; special purpose commodities are mainly imported from outside and are not imperative for the native way of life. In transactions involving general purpose commodities, such as rice, corn, oil, earthenware, baskets, leaf mats, vegetables, and ropes, the natives follow the traditional economic practices; with special purpose commodities, like tailored garments, mill-clothes, mirrors, cosmetics, and so forth, the natives follow the practices of modern self-regulating market economies.

The needs of a Budhua informant will illustrate the traditional economic practices of the region. On one occasion, this Budhua informant wanted to buy four pairs of ropes each ten-foot long for his cattle. He went to the Birhor at the market margins, but, as it was late in the afternoon, the Birhors had already sold most of their ropes, only two pairs remaining. Budhua asked their barter value in rice, and gave one Paila, approximately two pounds of rice in exchange. After finishing this deal, Budhua, still badly needing two pairs, and finding no more among the Birhors, reluctantly went to the market centre and purchased ropes imported by an urban trader. Budhua paid the trader fifty Naye Paise in cash. When I asked him why he had bartered with the Birhor and paid cash to the trader, he replied that one was a native and the other was alien; that is, one was a trade of a general purpose commodity and the other of a special purpose commodity.

The tribal people generally refrain from using cash, preferring barter in transactions involving regional products. For example, Somra Oraon was once making purchases for his son's wedding. He was carrying a basketful of rice and a container of clarified butter. He first went to a Māhli from whom he bought a native drum for twenty Pailas of rice; then he went to a Turi and purchased two bamboo baskets for one Paila of rice; then he went to a Birhor to buy two pairs of ropes for one Paila of rice; and then to a Chik-Baraik to purchase hand-woven cloth for which he gave about two pounds of clarified butter. He then went to an Asur and purchased two leaf rain-coats and nearly a hundred leaf cups for drinking rice beer, in exchange for three Pailas of rice. Somra still had about fifteen Pailas of rice which he took to a Phariya and sold for cash (five rupees). Proceeding to the market centre, he bought four plastic combs, two mirrors, and a bead necklace for cash. Although at first the practice of carrying a big basket of rice for shopping appeared cumbersome, it clearly indicated that Somra distinguished between commodities produced and sold by natives and those imported and sold by urban traders.

There are many tribesmen like Somra and Budhua who find greater satisfaction in buying local products rather than imported ones. When asked why they preferred ropes made by the Birhor to those imported from urban centres, natives invariably replied, "Although apparently the urban ropes are finer and smoother, the Birhor ropes are better." Similar responses were recorded for most of the other native commodities. Many tribesmen preferred the higher valued handwoven clothes of the Chik-Baraiks to the low-priced mill-made imported clothes. Some Oraons who had mill-clothes stated that they actually preferred hand-woven clothes but purchased mill-clothes because they were cheaper.

In innumerable instances the investigator found that the natives' cultural values overrode economic considerations. One informant, in whose house I lived for nearly three months, purchased every week two to four pieces of earthenware at the intertribal market. Once, when I calculated for him the price he had paid for these earthenwares, and suggested that he could have purchased a large aluminium ware of the same size which would have lasted much longer, for all that he had spent for the earthenware, he asked very seriously, "Do you think the kind of satisfaction you get from cooking food in earthenware can be had in any aluminium utensils?" Most tribesmen interviewed by the investigator shared this view. They thought, for example, that iron hoes made by the Asur and Lohra were far superior in performance to those imported from urban centres. As supporting evidence, an Oraon cited his neighbour's purchase of an imported hoe which had broken in about a week, justifying his faith in regional commodities. In general, the tribesmen preferred anything made by hand to that made by machine, small-scale handicrafts to large-scale machine-made goods.

In general, the tribes and castes of the region prefer to barter their commodities rather than sell them for cash. Several tribal informants stated that when they bartered commodities, they received some product in exchange for their own, but when they sold any commodities for cash they received something which had no immediately useful purpose : the intrinsic value of money made no sense to them. Although I never saw money being used as a commodity—that is, measured by volume in the native Paila as in other commodities—there were several evidences of such use in the past. Some informants told me that at the turn of the present century, when government agents went to collect revenues in the Banari market, the tribesmen paid their dues in coins as demanded by the agents—not, however, by counting them but by placing them in measuring cups, the Pailas. However, with the present use of barter in transactions of all regional commodities and the limited use of money for trading, only the purchase of urban commodities indicates that money serves a special purpose at the intertribal market.

The general purpose commodities which the natives produce in the region are bartered according to a traditionally fixed scale of relative values. A tribal or caste resident of the region knows that two pieces of earthenware can be exchanged for a Paila of rice, a bamboo basket for half a Paila, two pairs of ropes for one paila, or a handwoven cloth for ten Pailas. Both peasant and artisan commodities know the values of their commodities in relation to all other general purpose commodities ; for example, a Māhli basket-maker stated that one of his baskets would bring a half Paila of rice, or one Paila of corn, or five Pailas of puffed rice, or a quarter Paila of mustard oil, or a pair of ropes. He also pointed out that his basket was worth two shaves of his beard ; of course, for this, he had to accept deferment of the payment for several weeks. While preferences exist and are practised every week at the intertribal market, a tribe or caste man does occasionally find a situation in which he cannot directly barter his commodities for something he desires. In such situation he employs the technique of serial barter, which means the transfer of commodities through barter between two or more hands. Once a Birhor wanted to barter his ropes for an iron sickle sold by a Lohra; however, as the ropes were not acceptable to the Lohra, the Birhor first bartered his ropes for corn and then bartered the corn for the sickle.

At the intertribal market, since relative values of general purpose commodities are traditionally determined, the tribesmen generally show indifference to the market principle of supply and demand. On many occasions, individuals prefer to return home even with perishable commodities like vegetables and fruits rather than exchange them at a reduced rate.

Once when the intertribal market was about to close, I asked an Oraon woman to sell her guavas at a cheaper price, but she refused to do so. However, after my great insistence, she said, "Look, I will give you all this [showing some quantity] free, but I will sell to you at this price only." This was a typical tribesman's response even in 1960, when only a few yards away from the margins, at the market centre, the urban traders were operating on a strict principle of supply and demand.

III. Change from Native Economy to Modern Self-regulating Market Economy

While general purpose commodities reinforce the native economy and help establish economic interdependence among the tribes and castes of the region, as reflected in the intertribal market, it is the special purpose commodity(ies) which introduces urban economy in the region and extends its economic ties with the world beyond.

Most special purpose commodities entering the intertribal market are introduced by the urban traders. However, some—for example, lac and honey—are produced in the region. The natives do not use these commodities; they produce them for export to urban centres in exchange for general purpose commodities, such as salt, kerosene oil, and tobacco, which are not available in the region. In such exchanges, tribesmen deal with the urban traders direct. Until recently the few urban traders who visited the Banari intertribal market bartered or used money to obtain the special purpose commodities in exchange for their general purpose commodities. However, when the urban traders introduced special purpose commodities such as mill-clothes, tailored garments and metal utensils, money and other characteristics of a self-regulating market economy were gradually introduced at the intertribal market.

The great gulf between the economic behaviour of the urban traders and the native tribes and caste men called for a new role on the part of the Phariya, who now serves as an economic mediator between the natives and the urban traders, the former using barter and the latter money. The Phariya can also be considered as a native economic change agent, since his role is to facilitate exchange between the native economy and the market economy.

Phariyas are natives of the region, literate and conversant with both the indigenous and the urban ways of living; they exert constant pressure on the regional people to reinterpret in indigenous terms the intrinsic value of money in economic transactions in which they take part. The native tribesmen traditionally treat money as a kind of special purpose commodity. A Phariya, in order to facilitate transactions between the tribesmen and the urban traders, assists the tribesmen in interpreting the economic role of money as a common denominator between the value of their produce and their needs. He serves to stress the usefulness of money as a medium of exchange rather than as a commodity, and hence converts it from a special purpose to a general purpose category. As an economic change agent, the Phariya plays an important role in converting the regional economy from one of barter to a modern self-regulating market economy.

On one occasion, to cite an example of how a Phariya operates, one of my native informants, Mangra Oraon, wanted to buy machine-made cloth from an itinerant trader, but he had only rice to give in exchange, and this was unacceptable to the trader, who wanted only cash. At the same time, a newly arrived Hindu school teacher wanted to buy rice for cash but could not do so because the Oraon native who had the rice wanted corn in exchange. A Phariya, in his role of economic mediator, solved their problems. To fulfil this mediating role, a Phariya now sits regularly at a booth in the market place and exchanges cash for commodities and *vice versa*. On several occasions I

A view of the Market-Centre

Urban traders arriving by bus with their trade goods

Urban traders arriving by bike

Trade goods being transported on bullock carts

A Phariya arriving with his horse

Oraon owmen on way to the market

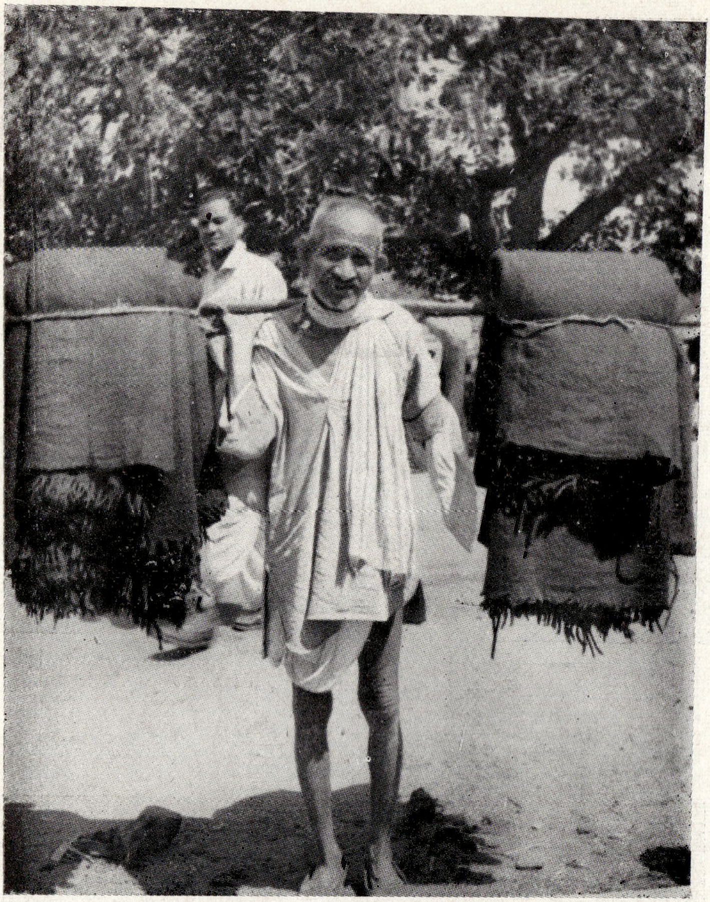

A Chik-Baraik weaver arriving with his blankets

Oraon men counting money received from the Phariya in exchange for rice

Pailas, measuring containers, being used for bartering commodities

Scales used for weighing green vegetables

An urban trader selling mill-made clothes

An urban trader selling hubble bubbles

Lohras, (ironsmiths) selling their implements

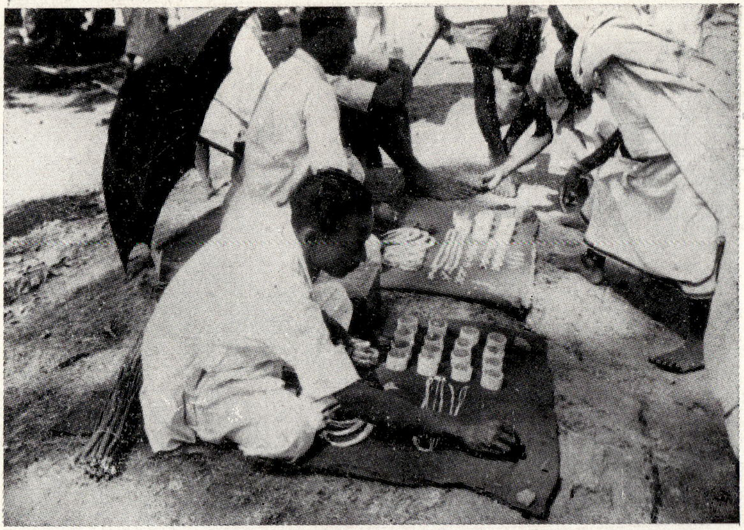

Silversmiths with their jewelleries

Asur women from hills selling leaf plates

Mahli, Basket-makers, sitting with their trade wares

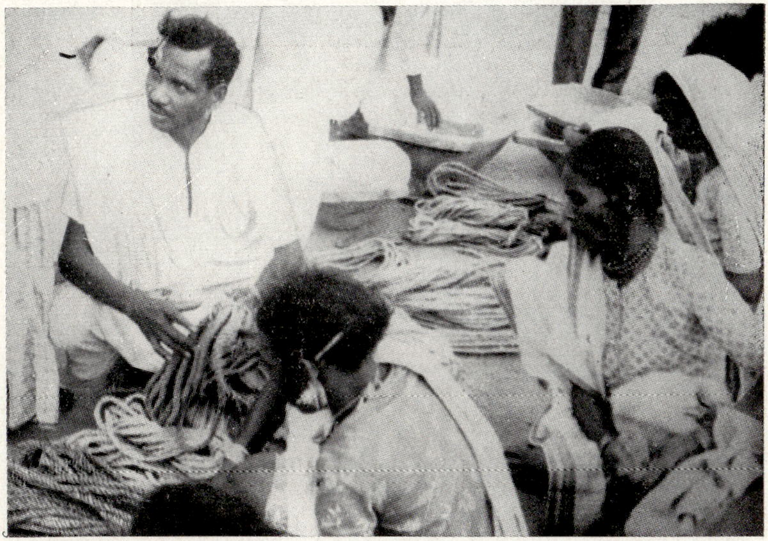

Birhor women selling ropes and wooden tubs

Chick-Baraik, weavers, displaying their handloom clothes

Potters occupying a section of the market place

Valley dwellers chatting and comparing brooms purchased at the market margins

A magician amusing the natives with cobra, a prelude to the sale of his magical charms and amulets

The Tana Bhagats, a reformist sect of the Oraons, holding a meeting at the market margins

A flute-seller from Lohardaga

A Woman selling spices

have resorted to a Phariya to buy native products, like drums, flutes, and pipes, which could not be obtained for cash. In changing cash for kind and *vice versa,* the Phariya functions somewhat like a modern bank where currencies of different countries may be exchanged.

A Phariya does not follow any prescribed rules. He creates his own rules, partly guided by his own idiosyncrasies and partly by his knowledge of the prices of commodities at nearby urban centres. Once Mangra Oraon wanted cash in exchange for a basket of rice so that he could buy a mirror from an itinerant trader. A Phariya gave him one rupee for the commodity and shortly thereafter sold it for one and a quarter rupee to a Hindu school teacher who wanted a basket of rice to buy a native drum. The Phariya earns a living by meeting the needs of such people as the Oraon and the Hindu school teacher and, in so doing, he introduces into the intertribal market the status and role of the middleman.

The Phariya brings to the tribal market other roles characteristic of a modern self-regulating market. Somra Māhli once brought a leaf mat to a Phariya, who gave him a rupee in exchange for it. A couple of weeks later, when he brought another leaf mat to the same Phariya, he was offered only three-quarters of a rupee. Somra did not understand this, since traditionally his mat would have had a fixed exchange value. The Phariya explained that not many people were now interested in buying this type of mat either in the tribal market or in the nearby urban centre where he marketed his surplus commodities. In other words, he implied that the demand for native mats had gone down and hence the value of the mat had declined. Somra accepted the explanation, assuming that the Phariya knew more about urban centres than he. Thus, in his role of middleman, the Phariya introduces to the tribal market the concept of price fluctuation in relation to supply and demand.

Somra Māhli recounted another experience with a Phariya, who reduced the price offered for a mat because its length was a few inches shorter than the standard. To Somra, such details as small variations in the size of a mat or the use of stained instead of perfect leaves seemed irrelevant to its exchange value. But to the Phariya, reflecting modern market attitude toward standardization of size and quality, these details are significant in determining market value.

The Phariya is responsible for many other innovations in the intertribal market. He visits urban centres and maintains direct contact with urban traders. He learns new things and introduces them in the intertribal market. At Banari, the tribes and caste men are accustomed to use wooden containers of different sizes for measuring commodities. This technique of measurement is not acceptable to the urban trader, nor is the use of standard weights and measures acceptable to the natives. Since the Phariya has to deal with both natives and urban traders, he keeps on hand a supply of measures suited to both peoples. One Asur told me how a Phariya had demonstrated to him the advantages of weights and measures over the indigenous containers, thereby inducing his acceptance of the novelty.

Two innovations introduced by the Phariya among the peoples of the region are of special interest. One Phariya, Ramnath, introduced the cultivation of potatoes to two native tribes, the Oraon and the Birjia. He supplied potato seeds to them without charge but on condition that they sell him the excess yield. The crop grew abundantly on the local soil and resulted in cash for the natives and rich dividends to Ramnath, both in prestige and in profits. Another Phariya, Ramadhin, introduced an improved technique of trapping monkeys among the Birhor, a tribe of monkey trappers. The new technique markedly influenced the economy of the Birhor and brought far-reaching consequences to their way of life (Sinha 1959 : 102).

In introducing modern market practices to the Banari intertribal market the Phariya, the native economic change agent, receives constant support from the trader, the urban economic change agent. Many Phariyas serve as agents to the traders. On one Monday in November 1959, it was observed that neither eggs nor clarified butter nor fine rice appeared for sale at the market place. Some Hindu residents, as well as urban teachers, revenue agents, searched for the eggs, butter, and rice everywhere at the market centre and the market margins, but they were not found until late in the afternoon when some urban traders put them up for sale at their booths in the market centre. An intensive inquiry later revealed that the urban traders had purchased all the commodities from the agriculturist tribes through the Phariyas. By creating an artificial scarcity, the urban traders had raised the price and thus introduced the technique of price fixing, so common in the self-regulating market economy.

By playing the role of money-lenders the urban traders have established a network of economic ties with the natives. Every advance of credit to the tribesmen incurs the obligation on their part to sell their surplus commodities to the urban traders. While a Phariya helps in establishing credits for the tribesmen, the urban traders introduce monopoly on some regional resources by making contacts with tribesmen via the Phariya in advance at the intertribal market. On several occasions, I have observed tribesmen from hills and valley seeking loans from urban traders direct for the purchase of agricultural implements, bullocks, and seeds, and for other minor purposes. Thus, through the urban traders and the Phariyas, the intertribal market offers loans and credit, serving as a kind of banking institution for the peoples of the region.

In 1958, the Government of India introduced decimal coinage and withdrew all old coins from circulation. Although the natives were not within reach of any state bank, the usual agent of exchange of official currencies, the urban traders provided substitutive facilities at the intertribal market. For months the traders exchanged the old currencies of the natives and, later, traded them with state banks in the course of their weekly visits to the urban centres. The traders bridged the gaps between the regional and the national economy.

Since 1953, the traders have introduced the modern market technique of advertising mass-produced special purpose commodities. At the Banari market advertising is a common phenomenon. To advertise the urban traders engage the Phariyas or specially trained persons transported from urban centres who display visual posters, sing especially composed songs on the commodity and distribute free samples. The most common special purpose commodities advertised are soap, Bidi (a cheap indigenous cigarette popular throughout India), match boxes and cosmetics.

The effectiveness of advertising is illustrated by the following example. An urban trader brought three young men from Lohardaga to advertise a brand of Bidi which he sold exclusively at the market place. One man had a harmonium, another a flute, and the third carried a bagful of Bidis. They had composed several songs elucidating various advantages of this brand. Two of the men sang and the third distributed samples to the natives. All three continued advertising almost all day, moving to various parts of the market place. At dusk when I asked the trader if he had been able to sell enough Bidis to cover the cost of advertising, he pointed towards the big cartoon of Bidis which was almost empty. By using advertising, the trader boosted his sales and influenced native preference for a special purpose commodity.

The intertribal market also serves as an informal employment exchange for natives as well as for state contractors who need labourers for various developmental projects in the region. On one occasion, when an urban contractor needed over seventy labourers, the Phariyas, who knew which natives were interested in seeking employment, helped in collecting the labour force. This practice has become so common that natives and contractors alike find the intertribal market an opportune place for negotiating employment.

IV

The cases presented above could be multiplied; however, from these data it is obvious that the intertribal market plays the dual role of maintaining economic interdependence among the communities in the region, and of changing the native economy to a modern self-regulating market economy. The intertribal market serves as a perfect mirror of the native economy. It indicates the nature and extent of native production and consumption of commodities, their surpluses and scarcities, and seasonal variations. It explains the native concept of economic behaviour, and it reveals also the kinds of urban commodities and economic characteristics which enter the region through it. The intertribal market reflects both centripetal and centrifugal forces, for it attracts native and urban commodities—both general and special purpose—and disperses them inside and outside the region.

CHAPTER VII

SOCIAL ROLE OF THE BANARI INTERTRIBAL MARKET

I

UNLIKE markets conceived in economic parlance as playing economic roles, the Banari intertribal market plays, in addition to such an economic role, social roles among the tribes and castes of the region. It functions as a centre of social life in the area. In the first place, it helps maintain the social entities within each tribal and caste group it serves; in the second place, it helps create a network of social ties among these groups; and in the third place, by providing entry points to what are subsequently referred to as "change agents," that is, urban traders, Phariya, development agents, and other specialists, it provides for and facilitates the process of social change in the region.

II. SOCIAL CONTINUITIES

In the spatial distribution of peoples at the market place, we find each tribal or caste group occupying roughly a distinct zone. By sharing the same zone, members of a tribe or caste, drawn from different villages in the region, find a ready-made opportunity for social "get-togethers." Kinsmen and clansmen discuss group welfare and other problems of mutual concern. Parents negotiate marriage of sons and daughters at the market place. While young boys and girls find the intertribal market the most suitable place for selecting their mates, and for courting, it is their parents who finally negotiate the marriage there. A tribal marriage involves a series of negotiations, including exchange of gifts and visiting the homes of both the parties, spread through several months (Roy 1915 : 184). The solution to the complicated procedure preceding marriage is facilitated through the intertribal market, where all parties can meet, discuss, and settle the details of the marriage negotiations, including gifts and visits.

In the winter of 1959, this investigator made a survey of marriage patterns among the villagers of Serandag, and it was found that seventy-eight out of eighty-one marriages were originated by either courtship or negotiations at the Banari intertribal market. The average distance between homes of the parties in a marriage in the above sample was seven miles, although in six cases it was thirteen miles. The survey revealed that 90 per cent of the couples used the intertribal market as the centre from which they moved back and forth to their parents' or in-laws' villages. On any market day one can observe several instances of parents handing over their daughters to the husbands' folks, or of husbands joining the groups of their in-laws to make social visits to their villages. This custom of visiting kinsmen has continued through generations, perhaps because travelling in small groups was difficult and dangerous in the region, but on market days, as villagers moved in large groups, it was safe to undertake any journey.

Some tribal groups find the intertribal market a convenient place to organize a Pachaura, a tribal council. As a rule such councils are organized only when some member transgresses tribal code. On one market day, I noticed a middle-aged Oraon carrying, in a distinctive way, a metal pitcher, walking up and down at the market margins. He would stop at intervals and inform tribal members that the Pachaura would be held on the next market day. Upon inquiry I was told that the metal pitcher symbolized the inviting of members to a tribal council. On the next market day nearly three hundred Oraon elders met in council in the mango grove near the market margins and decided to excommunicate a young Oraon who had transgressed the rules of a tribal endogamy by marrying a Māhli woman. Several months later, a Hinduized section of the Oraon, called the Tana Bhagats, organized a very big rally on market day; the rally also included sect members from outside the region. Meetings of a tribal council, especially of tribal elders, are held at intervals and sometimes take place so quietly that anyone not already aware of them would never know about them. Although I attempted to record every event of the market place, on several occasions I learned about tribal council meetings only after they were past.

An example of how social continuity and tribal unity operate at the market place may be relevant here. Once some individuals from a hill tribe, the Birjia, decided that it would be lucrative to make ropes for sale at the intertribal market. One Monday, three Birjia tribal members brought ropes to the market and occupied seats in the zone traditionally used by the Birhor rope-makers. Later, when some Birhors arrived, they asked the intruding Birjias to leave, but the Birjias refused. However, by noon, when all the Birhors gathered, they insisted on the Birjias to leave the zone. Anticipating serious trouble, the Birjias left and joined their tribesmen in the other section of the market margins. This incident showed how a tribal group would react when its basic securities were threatened.

III. Social Ties Among The Regional Groups at The Intertribal Market

One way in which the intertribal market extends social relationships among the tribal and caste groups of the region is by providing common grounds for social participation. To all peoples of the region every market day is a holiday. Men and women, young and old, look forward to the Monday intertribal market, when they expect "fun and frolics" mixed with social and economic business. On Sunday almost every individual in the region spends time in preparation for the market the following day. He washes clothes, for it is a native belief that one should be neatly dressed at the market ; he prepares commodities for exchange or sale at the market, and he contacts other neighbours who may travel to the market place in groups in order to join them. The peoples of the region call the Banari intertribal market, "Our market." The feeling of belonging to an intertribal market is shared by all the tribes and castes in the region.

One way in which social ties extend among the tribes and castes of the region is through the custom of intertribal, ceremonial friendships. Individuals from different parts of the region meet frequently at the intertribal market. In the course of time, some develop intimate friendships. This often leads to the formation of a common bond of ceremonial friendship among them, which involves mutual rights and obligations reinforced by periodic gift exchange (Tandon 1960 : 38). In my survey during the spring of 1959, it was observed that every adult man and woman had established ceremonial friendship with one or more persons belonging to a tribal or caste group of the region.

An intertribal market is also a centre of recreation for the peoples of the region. Many people visit the market merely to participate in regional sports. Cockfights, dance shows of bears and monkeys, trapeze shows and snake charming are some of the favourite sports which attract people from all tribes and castes of the region. The intertribal market likewise brings them together for beer drinking, which serves as a meeting place for the tribes and castes of the region.

Persons from all tribes and castes in Banari participate in the four regional festivals, called Sohrai, Sahrul, Fagua, and Karma. At any of these festivals, which are all celebrated on market days, one can observe the expression of regional unity at the intertribal market. Once while attending the Fagua festival at the Banari intertribal market, the investigator observed the following :

> It was noon when people began pouring into the market from different directions. The Māhlis were playing on drums. The Turis were playing flutes; the Birhors had brought their ropes for tricks; the Oraons and others were dancing in groups. Everyone was playing, dancing, and enjoying the occasion . . . Individuals from all the tribes and castes were drinking beer, making jokes, and dancing, as if they all belonged to a common whole.

One interesting and important role of the intertribal market is that of an indigenous channel of communication. The intertribal market serves as a kind of news service for the people of the region. Many tribesmen go to the market merely to collect news of relatives, friends, tribesmen, and of the region and world outside. The individuals who fail to attend a market often feel as we feel after missing the day's newspaper or a news-cast. In a region where no modern system of communication operates, the intertribal market is the only means of communication for the peoples. Even for the urban agents, such as postmaster, revenue peon, landlord, administrator, or welfare worker, an intertribal market is the best place and the best medium of contacting and communicating with the natives.

IV. Social Change at The Intertribal Market

Cases pointing to social unity of a tribal group or social solidarity of the region, as reflected through the intertribal market, are many. But let us examine here the contributions made by urban peoples—such as traders, government agents, community development workers, religious preachers, and political leaders—through their regular contacts with the intertribal market. Although the overt roles of these urban peoples vary greatly, as their professions indicate, all share and play, perhaps, even more important role of a social change agent, since each attempts to introduce his ideas, beliefs, and practices, which are certainly very different from those of the tribes and castes of the region.

Three kinds of social change agents may be distinguished in operation at the intertribal market. The first may be called a secular change agent, who deliberately or unknowingly changes the tribesmen's conceptions of the secular environment, such as officials of the public administration, school system, or political organization. The second is a religious change agent, who operates to change the native conception of the religious system, such as missionary, social reformers; the third, the economic change agent, a Phariya or an urban trader, who has the direct purpose of blending the native economy with the modern market economy, while his indirect role may be identified as that of facilitating social change in the region.

Secular change agent

The social roles of a secular change agent can best be explained by a few illustrative examples.

The system of police administration is alien to the traditional thought pattern of most tribesmen. Several years ago, when the government opened up a police station in the region, many tribal folks did not understand its functions. An informant told me that in the beginning the police officials did not understand the tribal peoples, nor did the latter understand the police. But the police officials continued visiting the intertribal market every week and took cognizance of any unlawful behaviour they noticed among the tribesmen. Because of his continuous presence at the intertribal market, the tribesmen gradually came to understand the functions of a police officer.

A revenue clerk of the state government uses the intertribal market to introduce the alien system of taxation on properties of the tribesmen. One finds a revenue clerk attending the market all the year round, contacting clients and collecting taxes. Once I noticed a peon of the revenue office issuing summons to several persons for the default of tax payments at the Banari market. The peon once informed the investigator that he had been able to serve fifty-seven summons—written notices—to tribesmen belonging to distant villages, in the course of a few hours at the intertribal market. Of course, it would have been impossible to deliver so many even in a week if he had had to serve the summons in the villages of the various clients. In his duties of serving summons the peon not only informs the tribesmen to appear at the revenue office for hearing, but also indirectly, but effectively, he creates among them a recognition of the nature of revenue administration, the strength behind the printed word, and the significance of literacy. In the role described above, the revenue clerk, or revenue peon, functions as a secular change agent.

Recently the federal communication service established a post office near the market place : one mailman is supposed to deliver mail to a large number of villages of the region. In general, not many tribesmen receive mail ; even then, it is physically impossible for one mailman to deliver promptly mail to all the scattered villages of the region. Hence, he uses the intertribal market to contact the addressees and deliver their mail. His very presence at the intertribal market tells the people that there is a communication system which connects the region to the world beyond. Several times when the mailman delivered letters to me at the Banari intertribal market, my Birhor and Asur friends asked who the man was and how he happened to bring letters from my home. When I explained the way the postal system worked, they were amazed, but certainly they learned something new. In this role, a mailman also serves as a secular change agent.

In 1956, the state government opened up an intensive programme for community development in the region. Trained specialists in agriculture, animal husbandry, cottage industries, public health and medicine, and irrigation, were brought to the region to implement this programme which can be considered as directed culture change. One extension agent in agriculture and another in cottage industries were stationed at Banari other specialists frequently visited the Banari intertribal market. They organized frequent demonstrations of modern techniques in agriculture, cottage industries, public health, and so on, and explained to the tribesmen the purpose of the community development programme. During several epidemic seasons, public health agents opened booths at the market for mass inoculations against cholera and smallpox. In the early phase of the community development programmes the tribesmen treated the extension agents as itinerant, urban advertisers, but in the course of time, through persistent demonstrations and contact at the intertribal market, the community development agents found some tribesmen who were receptive to new ideas.

The intertribal market helped these secular change agents not only to introduce modern implements or medicine but also modern concepts of public health and standards of living and, above all, to create among the tribesmen an awareness of the welfare state in which the government's responsibility is to assist them in development.

The tribal and even caste peoples of the Banari region have hardly been aware of the political organizations which govern the whole country. In the fall of 1956 I made a random survey of the intertribal market to find out how many people were aware of even persons like Mahatma Gandhi, the father of the Indian nation, Pandit Nehru, then the prime minister, and the Congress party, India's ruling party. This purely random survey revealed that only 3 per cent had heard of Gandhi, 3.5 per cent knew Nehru, and only 1 per cent identified the Congress party. However, in the winter of 1958, the figures had risen to 8.5 per cent for Gandhi, 21 per cent for Nehru, and 18 per cent for the Congress party. Also, 31 per cent of the tribesmen knew of another political party called Jharkhand, which had been organized during 1957 general election to represent the cause for the tribes of Central India. I personally witnessed several political rallies organized by the candidates for the Congress, the

Jharkhand, and other parties.

Once, when a leader of the Jharkhand party came to the Banari market to open the campaign, he addressed a crowd of about three thousand tribesmen and explained his political manifesto which was composed as a folksong. A leaflet, which was distributed to the tribesmen, contained the words of the song and showed a picture of a cock, the symbol of the party. This song became so popular that tribal peoples sang it on every market day for several months subsequently. Without any further effort or other form of canvassing than his folksong, this candidate got free publicity throughout the region, and was ultimately elected by an overwhelming majority. To such political candidates, who are actually secular change agents, the intertribal market offers a ready-made audience for communicating their views and influencing the people. Incidents were frequently witnessed during the election season at the intertribal market, which not only made the tribesmen aware of the political parties operating in the region but also educated them as to the nature of the larger political structure of the state and the country of which they are a part. The tribesmen gradually learned to want to participate in the democratic process of election and subscribe to the idea that every adult man and woman has a right to vote, a right which seems so alien and yet so prestige-giving to them.

Another incident may indicate how the intertribal market is used by secular change agents to formulate opinion on legislation affecting the natives. In the summer of 1959, members of a political party came to the Banari market and appealed to the peoples of the region to protest against state legislation on consolidation of land holdings. The visitors, in a general speech, indicated that this legislation would alienate people's rights on their land, and they requested that they sign or print a thumb impression on an application to the state government, which was being circulated at the market, to rectify the situation. Although it was difficult to estimate the number of tribes or castemen who understood the nature of the appeal, nearly four hundred thumb impressions and a dozen signatures were put on the forms.

The school teachers from the schools in the region also play the role of secular change agents at the intertribal market.

Schools are usually closed on market days, and frequently the teachers bring their students to the market in groups, perhaps as a technique of inviting the people's interest and participation in formal schooling. On one occasion I noticed the school boys were brought to the market each carrying placards on "health week." The boys, led by the school teachers, were shouting slogans on health and personal hygiene.

On another occasion school children were brought to the market to demonstrate techniques of fire prevention in the forests. The forest range officials, police, and school teachers had jointly organized this demonstration. Subsequent interviews with tribesmen revealed that this demonstration had not only shown novel techniques of five prevention but had also indicated how school children were developing into useful persons.

Religious Change Agent

The roles of religious change agents are evidenced by the introduction of alien religious beliefs and attitudes among the tribesmen. Some agents make open efforts; others make indirect impact; but in either case use is made of the intertribal market. For the expression of their views a few illustrations may indicate the role of the intertribal market in this social process.

Several years ago the landlord of Banari built a Hindu temple at the market place. When I asked why he had chosen that particular site, he replied : "It is centrally located. Everyone comes to the market place, and even those who do not believe in religion [meaning the tribal folks] may see God [image] without extra effort." Although among Hindus it is considered a sacred deed to build a temple, the choice of the site at the Banari market reflects the underlying motives of the Hindu landlord. On every market day a Brahmin priest makes an offering at the temple and then distributes it to tribes and castemen who pass by. On several occasions I noticed small groups of bards—Hindu folk singers—playing the harmonium and singing selections from Hindu epics, moving up and down at the market place. While the bards make their living by travelling around the country and singing songs, by visiting this market they were diffusing Hindu religious beliefs among the tribesmen : both the Hindu landlord and the Hindu bards performed the role of religious change agents.

In the winter of 1959, urban traders circulated a pamphlet which predicted the end of the world at 12 o'clock midnight on the fourteenth day of March. This was a statement and prediction made by Hindu astrologers from northern India. The pamphlet also described the rituals and worship everyone should perform in order to avoid this catastrophe. A few literate Oraons, who happened to read the pamphlet, circulated the rumour by word of mouth. Within seconds everyone at the market was taking about it. Some tribesmen were frightened and expressed deep anxieties. As a consequence, one could see on the Monday before March fourteenth groups of tribesmen making offerings at the Hindu temple. The event perhaps engendered among the tribesmen vague ideas about Hindu astrology. By introducing the pamphlet at the intertribal market, the urban trader served as religious change agent.

The intertribal market is also used by Protestant missionaries to preach their faith and recruit followers. Once during the winter of 1959, a European missionary visited the Banari intertribal market with half a dozen converts who were trained to sing selections from the Holy Bible translated into the Kurukh and the Sadani dialects. The missionary played the harmonium, and the converts sang. Wherever they stopped at the market centre and margins, large crowds of tribesmen surrounded them. After every song the European missionary gave a brief talk on Christianity in the Kurukh or Sadani dialect, which amazed many tribesmen. Although it was difficult to estimate the influence of the European missionary on the religious beliefs of the tribesmen, he may well have served as a religious change agent.

The intertribal market is the centre of a bi-monthly congregation of a Hinduized sect of the Oraon tribe, called Tana-Bhagats, which promises a better world for the tribal folk. Leaders of this sect sometimes preach the tenets of their faith and invite natives to join them, thus functioning as religious change agents. Their meetings expose many natives to religious viewpoints held by the reformist sect.

Economic Change Agent

While the economic role of an economic change agent is directly observable, as we saw in the last chapter, his implicit social role is perhaps even more important. When a Phariya, a native economic change agent, converts an individual's commodity into cash, he is not merely engaging in an economic transaction but translating urban values into the local idiom; for he is transmitting the alien concept of money to the people. Traditionally, tribesmen exchanged only objects which had a visible use, such as rice, mats, or drums; but now the Phariya exchanges these for a coin or a paper bill which has only intrinsic value, acting as a medium of exchange, as a measure and standard of value, and as a means of storing wealth.

A Phariya also functions as an informal news agency at the tribal market. His booth is located beside the lanes and paths which converge at the market place. He observes everyone who passes and converses with most of them. He listens to news and stories from some and passes them on to others. On one occasion a Phariya was told that a high government officer was expected to visit the Banari market the following week, and within the course of an hour everyone at the market place knew of the intended visit. On another occasion a postman, who was looking for a native named Khaira Oraon but did not know how to find him, mentioned his problem to a Phariya; the latter instituted a word-of-mouth search, and in about ten minutes Khaira appeared. By virtue of his contacts with the hinterland, a Phariya can send message widely. I once wanted to meet the chief of a particular Birhor settlement and mentioned this to a Phariya; he immediately sent word through a Birhor individual who happened to be available, and the chief himself appeared the next day. By collecting and disseminating news, the Phariya functions as a medium of communication where almost no modern system exists. Government agents, urban traders, and other urban people find it profitable to establish contacts with Phariyas in order to communicate with tribesmen and to obtain news of the hinterland.

Being aware of government procedures, a Phariya can interpret them to tribesmen and sometimes even act on their behalf. A native named Budhua Oraon, on receiving a notice from a government agent which he was unable to read, took it to a

Phariya, who not only read, translated, and interpreted it to him but also advised him what action to take.

A Phariya knows the resources both of the government and of the natives. By virtue of his contacts he usually knows the right person to get in touch with. Thus he often guides tribesmen to government agents who can provide the kinds of help that the state is offering the hill tribes. I observed a number of cases of illness in which a Phariya suggested to tribesmen that they try the western medicine which the government made freely available. Some found it helpful, with the result that a noticeable change occurred in the attitude toward alien medicine. In 1958, a community development agent wanted to introduce certain modern agricultural techniques among the tribesmen but was unsuccessful in several cases. He mentioned his problem in the course of a conversation with a Phariya, who directed him to several tribesmen whom he knew to be receptive to new ideas. When the agent established contact with them, they proved ready to accept the innovations. Cases of the sort described occur repeatedly.

V

From the data presented in the last three sections, several prominent facts emerge. The social role of the Banari intertribal market is three-fold : one, it helps maintain social identity of the tribe and caste groups of the region ; two, it assists in creating and continuing regional social unity ; and three, it is a medium for introducing social change in the region. A group of secular, religious, and economic change agents are active in bringing about social change at the intertribal market.

Chapter VIII

ONE TRIBE IN RELATION TO THE BANARI INTER-TRIBAL MARKET : THE CASE OF THE BIRHOR

In the preceding chapters I have examined the socio-economic roles of the Banari intertribal market among the tribal and caste communities of the hinterland. In this chapter I propose to examine how intricately the socio-economic life of one tribal community of the region, namely, the Birhor, is interwoven with the Banari intertribal market.

The Birhors are a semi-nomadic community of food gatherers, hunters, and rope-makers who make their living on the resources from forests. Of about 2,500 Birhors in Chota Nagpur in 1956, there were nearly three hundred living in five aboriginal settlements of this region. An aboriginal settlement of the Birhor is called Tanda. A Tanda constitutes a minimal patrilineage comprising five to eight nuclear families and on an average of thirty persons (Sinha 1958 : 87). Each family in a Tanda occupies a conical leaf-hut of about five feet in diameter, which is erected by the members of a family in a few hours. Wild leaves and twigs are the only materials required to erect a leaf-hut Kumba. A Tanda is a unit of Birhor social organisation. It is generally located at the outskirts of forests, in comparative isolation from other tribes and castes of the region. The only place where Birhors come into contact with outsiders is the intertribal market where they barter, exchange or sell ropes, manufactured from wild fibres, tubs made of wood, honey, and wild flowers collected from the forest, and hides of monkeys hunted in the woods. These are exchanged for rice, salt, oil, clothes, and other consumer goods. Of their isolation Dalton (1879 : 158) wrote, "they [Birhor] are seldom seen in the village [of other tribes], but the women frequent the markets to sell their rope and jungle produce." Another ethnographer, writing in 1888 (Driver 1888: 14), states: "Their [Birhor] women help them to make chop string, and also carry this and monkey skins to the village market situated nearest to the jungles, and there either sell or barter their articles for rice, salt, and oil. The skins of monkeys are used for making Kol [tribal] drums." There are other accounts on the tribe (Risley 1911 : 33); (Roy 1925 : 41), which describe their isolation and also their contacts with other peoples through intertribal markets.

I

The culture of the Birhor hinges on one hand on the forest and on the other on the intertribal market. A Birhor Tanda migrates from one site to the other at an interval of six months to five years. The migration is determined primarily by two factors : dwindling of forest resources, and decline in local demand for their commodities at the intertribal market. Although I did not get a chance to see an actual migration of a Tanda during 1959-61, interviews revealed that the above two factors were responsible for their migration and also for selection of a new settlement site.

The Birhors live on subsistence economy. Wild roots and fruits and the meat of trapped monkeys and other small animals are the only consumption goods they produce. Ropes and wooden tubs are manufactured by them to cater to the needs of neighbouring tribes and castes. As these make an important part of the economy and need to be traded in order to secure basic necessities for existence, the intertribal market offers an effective institution for the Birhor.

The forest economy of the Birhor creates great physical strain on the group. The collection of roots and fruits, honey, and wax is seasonal, the hunting of animals is uncertain, and cutting wood is a difficult enterprise for the Birhor who have simple technology of axe and adze. These put much premium on their time. Sometimes weeks elapse and yet they have hardly gotten any return from their efforts in the forest. In their weekly-cycle it has been observed that they spend four to five days in the forests, one day in the intertribal market, and the rest in preparation of the marketable commodities. Where people have hardly time to trade their commodities by visiting neighbouring villages, as is the case in some parts of India, the intertribal market provides them a ready-made place for trading their commodities in a short period of time. It serves as a pivot of their primitive economy.

The forests in the Banari region are spread over hundreds of square miles. It is difficult—rather impossible—for a small group of Birhor to keep track of game and forest produce in different localities. At the intertribal market they meet people from all parts of the region and collect information on the availability of forest resources. Especially when they engage in monkey-hunting expeditions, which require a score of men and nets, they find the intertribal market an easy avenue to contact persons from different Tandas and organize collective hunts. In 1959, several proposals of collective hunts originated at the Banari intertribal market, which I had the opportunity to record.

A Birhor from the Banari region regularly visits the intertribal market, where he has a fixed zone in the market region. There he sits, and sells or exchanges commodities. The presence or absence of a Birhor, as also the number and kind of commodities he brings to the market, reflect his economic condition. On several occasions in the monsoon, it was observed that only four or five Birhors came to the market place. Interviews revealed that others from their Tanda were still in the forest trying to collect resources that could be exchanged at the market place. The seasonal variation in their economy can also be gauged through the market. They bring for exchange or sale various kinds of ropes and strings and wooden tubs in the summer; and honey, wax, monkey skins in the winter. As the forests do not yield sufficient produce in monsoon, very few of their commodities enter the market.

Sometimes when their commodities are not sold at the Banari market, the Birhors walk down to other intertribal markets outside the region. This is necessary primarily because they do not adjust their prices according to the modern economic principle of supply and demand. In the monsoon of 1958-59 the Birhor of the Banari region faced a serious economic crisis. Some of them travelled fifteen to twenty miles on foot to sell their commodities at other intertribal markets. This situation was created by an influx of mass-manufactured ropes by the urban traders at the intertribal market. Virtually at the point of starvation, the Birhor of the region decided to migrate, but in time the state welfare officer intervened. The state purchased all the ropes manufactured by the Birhor for the next few months and eased their economic difficulties.

At the intertribal market a Birhor carries on economic transactions with other tribes and castes of the region on the basis of a traditionally fixed scale of relative values of commodities. A ten-and-a-half yard rope fetches two Pailas (approximately two pounds) of rice, four Pailas of maize, five Pailas of Gondli, wild rice, and, of late, 36 Naye Paise (approximately 5 naye paise make a cent) in cash. Special kinds of ropes manufactured at the requests of individuals at the market have also a fixed set of prices. A wooden tub is exchanged for ten Pailas of rice, a monkey hide for a pair of loin-cloth for men or women. In 1958, when an urban trader was contacted, the Birhor discovered a new market for live monkeys. The trader suggested that he was interested in buying live monkeys, trapped by them in the forests. He had to export them to some national laboratories for research, and he advanced cash to the head men of the Birhor Tandas, ensuring supplies of all trapped monkeys to him in the future. Through this single contract at the Banari intertribal market, this urban trader, an economic change agent, introduced the concepts of credit and cash among the Birhor. The effects of these have been analysed elsewhere (Sinha 1959).

The material culture of the Birhor is quantitatively simple. A nuclear family owns one or two baskets or winnowing fans made by the Māhlis and Turis of their region; two or three earthenwares made by Hindu potters for storing water, cooking cereals or fermenting rice beer; a couple of bottles for storing oil; mirror and comb; wooden tubs for storing wild roots, fruits and cereals; an iron axe for cutting wood and creepers, and several nets (the largest is thirty by six feet and the smallest six by two feet) for trapping monkeys, hares, porcupines, and other small animals. In one Tanda, one Birhor had a spade and a sickle and another had a knife and a pair of scissors, the latter used for cropping hair. Several young girls had tailored blouses, some boys had banians, and a few children had shorts and jackets. In another Tanda two young men owned scarves, and three girls had glass bangles and eyeliners. Some women owned nickel ornaments, necklaces, earrings, and rings. Others had earrings made of palm-leaves. A quick look at these possessions of the Birhors, however, indicates that most of these are acquired by the Birhors from other tribes and castes of the region and outside intertribal markets.

The semi-nomadic Birhor generally do not domesticate animals other than dogs. Occasionally they raise poultry. Some of them stated that in times of need it was easier to sell fowl and eggs than rope and strings at the intertribal market. One Birhor had regular contact with an urban trader to supply eggs weekly. In return he could at any time borrow cash or kind from the trader.

II

In the life cycle of a Birhor, the intertribal market is as important as in their economic life. Like many other societies, among Birhor the birth of a child is an occasion of great joy. All the members of a Tanda celebrate the arrival of a new member on the sixth day, which is called Chatti. However, when the resources do not permit immediate festivity, they celebrate the event at any time during the first year. On this occasion it is obligatory for a Birhor to invite maternal relatives of the child and his own paternal relatives. Since a Birhor always lives hand-to-mouth, trying to accumulate food provisions for the next day, he hardly finds time to visit his relatives or invite them personally. Here he takes advantage of the intertribal market, from where he sends invitations to relatives by word of mouth. He also entertains them at the intertribal market on an appointed day. During the winter of 1959 I observed the birth ceremony of a Birhor at Serka Tanda. Budhua, whose wife delivered a baby, came to the Banari intertribal market on Monday and announced the birth to his tribesmen. He, along with other elders of his Tanda, decided to celebrate the occasion on the following Monday market day. He sent word to his relatives through people present at the market, asking them to join in the celebration. On the next Monday four pitchers of rice beer were brought to the intertribal market by the members of the Budhua's Tanda. Budhua brought a chicken for sacrifice to ancestral spirits and purchased tobacco for offering to the guests. In the late afternoon all the Birhors gathered in one corner of the market margins, sacrificed chicken and drank rice beer, ceremonially offered by Budhua. The mother's brother—the uncle of the child—brought a hand-loomed dress for the child's mother. Other guests brought gifts of rice, pulse and salt. The ceremony lasted hardly an hour, although people stayed around for several hours. Later, I was told by the Birhors that they no longer used intertribal market for celebrating life events. However, this illustration may indicate the usefulness of the market place in the life cycle of the Birhor.

Marriage is considered the second important event in the life of a Birhor. It takes place only when two persons of the opposite sex decide to undertake responsibilities for an independent household. A young man is married to a girl only when he has accumulated enough resources to afford expenses of the formal ceremony. Although there are contributions made by the members of one's Tanda for celebrating a marriage, a Birhor man has to spend nearly one hundred rupees on his marriage ceremony. Besides the bride price of seven rupees, he has to pay for the feast for the relatives, to buy dress for the bride, the bride's mother, the bride's brother, and himself; and a necklace, bangles and a ring for the bride at the intertribal market. As celebrating marriage presents a difficult financial problem to a Birhor, he generally marries a girl only after they have lived together for several years. Data on marital alliance revealed that twenty-nine out of thirty-six marriages were performed one or more years after a couple began living together as husband and wife. In most cases a young man had met a girl at the intertribal market and after a series of contacts they decided to live together. An informal permission from the parents is enough for the social approval. Of thirty-six marriages studied, all of them had originated at the intertribal market, twenty-eight among unmarried boys and girls, six among unmarried boys and married women, and two among divorced men and married women.

Cases of elopement of married women with unmarried men from the intertribal market are not infrequent among the Birhor. In the course of a year, four such cases were witnessed. One may illustrate the situation. Somra, a thirty-two-year old Birhor, was married to an eighteen-year-old girl Budhni. Somra was lazy, he could not support his wife; consequently, she was unhappy. Budhni once met Chatarpal, a young man from another Tanda at the Banari intertribal market. In the course of weeks they developed a strong acquaintance, and one market day they met and eloped from the market place. They spent two weeks in the forest. Later Chatarpal brought her to his Tanda, and there they lived together. This precipitated conflict between the two Tandas, about which I will talk later.

Some Birhor marriages are arranged by negotiations between the parents of the bride and the groom. In such cases they also utilize the intertribal market for conducting the negotiations.

As in marriage, so in death the Birhor utilize the intertribal market. Unlike the marriage ceremony, death rites among Birhors cannot be postponed. Within a week the news of death has to be communicated to the relatives and members of the clan inside and outside the region. These messages are communicated through persons attending the intertribal markets. On the ninth day after death, the clan elders assemble at the Tanda and perform rituals which may place the dead in the category of ancestor spirit. Every relative brings gifts in kind : rice, pulse, rice beer, and so forth, which are added together for the death feast. Although these rituals are always held in a Tanda, I was told that those relatives who cannot attend the ceremony personally must later be entertained with rice beer at the intertribal market.

III

The pattern of nomadism of a Birhor Tanda is more or less stable and yet the two-and-a-half thousand Birhors hardly know of all the Tandas of the tribe. There are less than seventy Tandas in Chota Nagpur, spread in an area two hundred miles long from Hazaribagh to Singbhum, but the Birhors of Banari know only eight Tandas outside their region. Ordinarily a Birhor knows only those of his tribesmen whom he meets at the intertribal markets.

A Birhor Tanda is related primarily to one intertribal market, but occasionally its members visit neighbouring markets to sell commodities, meet friends, relatives, and clansmen. Intertribal contacts among the Birhors are maintained through a chain of intertribal markets. The Birhors of Banari sometimes visit the Adar intertribal market, twelve miles south-east, and the Tendar intertribal market, ten miles west. I was told that Birhors from Banari, Tendar, and Palkot, farther west, occasionally meet at the Tendar intertribal market and establish contacts.

Although a Birhor Tanda is an independent social entity, where disputes between two or more Tandas arise, tribal elders from several Tandas are invited to settle these disputes. For such purposes, an intertribal market is selected where they meet, discuss, and resolve the dispute. In the already cited case of elopement of Somra's wife with Chatarpal, a meeting of the elders from five neighbouring Tandas was called by members of Somra's Tanda. One Monday at the Banari intertribal market, the tribal elders assembled to discuss the dispute. As Somra insisted that his wife be returned to him, and as his wife was not willing to return, the dispute could not be resolved. The tribal elders then decided to invite people from several Tandas outside the region. Two weeks later the meeting was called at the Tendar intertribal market, where it was decided that Chatarpal, who had eloped with Somra's wife, should return to Somra the amount that he had spent on her marriage.

A Birhor Tanda is always located in forests, distant from other habitations. And the Birhor usually refer their location in relation to the intertribal markets they visit. Once when I asked a Birhor chief about the locations of his past settlements, he replied, "I was born here and have since moved to Tendar, Chainpur, Palkote, Chakradharpur, Adar, Jamti, Manatu and Mudar." All these names are places where intertribal markets are held. Probing interviews revealed that he had camped and lived at some other places near these markets, but he thought such a settlement could best be identified by the markets associated with it. It is interesting that Birhors tell their life histories with reference to the intertribal markets they have known in the past. As the Birhors are preliterate, their important events such as birth, marriage, and death are calculated by their recounting associations with the markets at the time of the incident. The Birhors' knowledge of time and space is greatly influenced by the intertribal markets.

The Birhors are considered the most primitive tribe of Chota Nagpur (Roy 1925 ; Vidyarthi 1958), and yet they are not a self-sufficient community. The list of material equipment of a Birhor family enumerated earlier indicates how much dependent they are on other communities. This dependence—rather interdependence—is clearly manifested at the Banari intertribal market where a Birhor sells or barters his commodities, ropes, monkey hides, wooden tubs, honey, and wax, for rice, maize, and other grains to the agricultural Oraon, Munda, and Kisan tribesmen; for clothes to the Chik-Baraik weavers; for earthenwares to the Kumhar potters; for baskets to the Māhli and the Turi basket makers; for iron axes to the blacksmith Lohra; and for several urban commodities to the urban traders. The occupational specialty of the Birhor gives them a distinctive identity at the intertribal market and brings them into contact with other tribes and castes of the region. Through recurrent economic transactions, some Birhors also establish permanent economic ties with other peoples at the market. S. C. Roy, the most noted ethnographer of the Birhor, has elaborately described how some Birhors have taken to permanent settlement and agricultural occupation at the influence of some agriculturist tribes and castes (Roy 1925 : 31). In Banari I have recorded half a dozen cases of Birhor young men who worked as labourers during the monsoon for agriculturist Oraon and Hindus of the region. Interviews with these individuals revealed that they had established contacts with their patrons at the intertribal market, who offered them employment in the monsoon when their traditional craft produced little result.

Some of the Birhors of the Banari region are famous as sorcerers and witch doctors. Although they follow their traditional occupation, sorcery and witchcraft fetch them supplementary income as well as prestige among the tribes and castes of the region. The Birhor sorcerers are known for curing men and animals, as well as inflicting disease on them. In order to make themselves available to the people of the region the Birhor sorcerers regularly attend the Banari intertribal market. On several occasions I have noticed Oraon, Munda, Kisan, and other tribesmen contacting the sorcerers at the market place. In some instances a sorcerer reads an omen for his client at the market; at other times he visits the client at his settlement to diagnose and prognose the ailing individual. Although I have never witnessed any instance of a sorcerer inflicting evil influence on any enemy of his clients, I was told by several persons that the Birhors practised this art as well. In any case, the intertribal markets help the sorcerer to practise his art.

One of the ways by which the Birhors, like all other tradesmen, extend their intertribal ties is by establishing ceremonial friendship at the intertribal market. This age-old practice of intertribal ceremonial friendship has been considered by several ethnographers of Central Indian tribes as an important means by which the tribesmen ensure security and hospitality in an inaccessible region (Roy 1925 : 269 ; Tandon 1960 : 58) Some of the Birhors of Banari reported ceremonial friendship with Oraon, Birjia, Asur, Māhli, and Hindu castes who lived in different parts of the region. It was reported by every informant that such friendship had originated at the market place In some cases, I was told, such friendships (which of course are among members of the same sex) gave entree to an individual in other tribal groups which led to intertribal marital alliance. Although tribal elders do not approve of this, in the Banari region one Birhor young man had married an Oraon girl and two Oraon men had married Birhor women. These affairs had started at the Banari intertribal market.

So far I have attempted to delineate some aspects of the intricate relationship that the Birhors reflect with the intertribal market. In the above accounts one may observe an all-pervading influence of the market in the Birhor socio-economic life. In 1956, when I first visited the Birhor of the Banari region, they were basically in an aboriginal state, living in leaf-hut Tandas, practising traditional occupations, and maintaining interdependent and intricate relationship with other tribes and castes of the region (Sinha 1958 ; 1963). The same year, fifteen families of the Birhor were brought together from two different Tandas by the Government and resettled permanently at Jehan Gutua, four miles east of Banari. In 1957, twenty-eight families from three other Tandas were resettled at another place, Benti, two miles west of Banari. Each nuclear family was given a two-room ventilated house, and five acres of land for cultivation and some agricultural implements to start a new way of life. Machines for manufacturing ropes were provided to the settlers and doles were given to every family for several months until they expected to harvest their first crop. This resettlement scheme had far-reaching consequences in the lives of the Birhors, which I have dealt with elsewhere (Sinha 1959). The cash doles the Birhor received brought them into effective transactions with urban traders at the intertribal market. Within only a few weeks they had purchased ready-made garments, mill-clothes, shoes, chappals, coloured glasses, cosmetics, and various other novelties. It appeared as if their repressed desires for urban novelties had been let loose. Later the rope-making machines helped them to manufacture many more ropes than they had ever made by hand. Over-abundance of ropes decreased their demand at the intertribal market. The Birhors then walked to other intertribal markets, fourteen to twenty miles away, to sell the ropes ; but when the demand declined, they returned to Banari, reduced the price, and sold wholesale to the urban traders at the intertribal market. This created among the Birhors an awareness of the market principle of supply and demand, to which I have referred earlier.

The introduction of agriculture engendered novel economic situation for the Birhors. Initial investment in land for reclamation, seeds and tools created reed for credit. The Government supplied some but seldom on time ; the urban traders at the Banari market found opportunities for investments and the Birhors gradually became clients to their loan business.

These resettlement schemes for the Birhor were widely publicized by the Government. Although the Birhors did not wholly like the idea of permanent settlement and agricultural occupation, the neighbouring tribesmen often commented regarding the preferential treatment offered to them by the Government. At the intertribal market the Birhors attracted a great deal of attention from all the people—from inside and outside the region. Almost everyone visiting the region from urban centres wanted to see and interview the Birhors at the intertribal market. A special officer for Birhor resettlement was appointed by the State, and stayed several miles away from the resettlement sites but always contacted the Birhors at the intertribal market to discuss their problems and prospects. A school was started at the resettlement site ; a social worker stayed with the Birhors for several months. This programme of directed change among the Birhor by the Government was greatly speeded up by the intertribal market, where the urban traders introduced every commodity—from papers and pencils, urban dress and cheap ornaments, to new implements—which was acceptable to them.

Chapter IX

THE STUDY OF THE BANARI INTERTRIBAL MARKET AND ITS CONTRIBUTIONS TO CONCEPTS AND THEORIES OF CULTURE CHANGE

I

Robert Redfield (1960 : 13) once commented :

> African societies lead the anthropologists away from the self-contained primitive community in a variety of respects . . . I am thinking of the large markets, system of production and distribution including thousands of people from wide-spread and, in cases, culturally different origins. Apparently no anthropologist has yet studied such a market system completely.

The above statement from a distinguished anthropologist of this century holds true not only for the African societies but also for many societies in other parts of the world. But, as I pointed out earlier, in Chapter I, none of the studies of tribal or peasant markets have explored non-economic or para-economic aspects of this institution. This dissertation, without pretending to make a complete study of any market, has attempted to explore and examine both economic and social dimensions of the Banari intertribal market in Chota Nagpur, India. If the result of this investigation does nothing else, it should dispel the naive notion that tribal or peasant markets can be properly understood without examining their social ramifications.

My aim in the present study has been to illustrate rather than to enumerate the roles of the Banari intertribal market. This has been done in the background of the ecological (Chapter III) and ethnic (Chapter IV) components of its hinterland, in the light of its folk and recorded history (Chapter V), and, above all, with reference to its actual operation, on Mondays, once a week, all year round as observed during 1957-61.

Also, I have shown how the Banari intertribal market operates in the complex ecological and cultural environment of the region. The ecological variation between the margins and centre of the Banari region, which are reflected in the types of resources they yield and the cultural variation between the margins and centre as expressed in the primitive and peasant communities living in the region, find in the intertribal market a centre of socio-economic interaction. In my review of the history and functioning of the Banari market (Chapter V), I have demonstrated how the institution of the intertribal market has been instrumental in bringing together and integrating the hill tribes and peasant communities into the regional culture of Banari. The age-long contact and socio-economic interaction among the peoples at the intertribal market has not levelled the cultural variations in the region. Rather, the data indicate that the socio-economic identity of a tribe has been as important for the functioning of the intertribal market as their socio-economic interdependence. The situation which results raises an important but still unresolved theoretical question with regard to cultural contacts and cultural change. Although not central to the issue of this dissertation, let me recall the comments of Horskovits (1955 : 482), who once wrote on the possible effects of contacts :

> Contact can result in minimal borrowing with or without external pressure, or it can range to almost complete acceptance of the ways of life of another people.

Although this statement can hardly be refuted, the field material from Banari further indicates that cultural contact can also create cultural interdependence, or, to use another term, intercultural balance (Thompson 1961 : 125). Honigmann (1959 : 256) uses the term "mutual respect" to define this aspect of acculturation. Much as this aspect of acculturation at Banari seems rewarding to investigate from a theoretical point of view, it did not come to my mind until I had left the field.

However, on the basis of this inquiry it would seem reasonable to advance the following hypothesis for further testing :

> Different ethnic groups can live in a region and share a regional culture through regular or recurrent contact at a focal point of that region and yet maintain their own parti-

cular, distinctive cultures. The sharing of a regional culture, however, and its continuing equilibrium is dependent on the particular contribution each of the component ethnic groups makes to the whole. Such equilibrium is likely to be disrupted through contact from outside the region at the point of contact, that is, the focal point of the regional culture.

—Hypothesis I

II

In the contemporary situation, the Banari intertribal market brings together peoples, not only from the tribal and peasant communities of the hinterland, but also members from urban communities who interact with each other regularly from their bases in the urban, trade and administrative centres of Chota Nagpur. This situation of culture contact between peasant and urban folk may be described as acculturation, or *culture change in process.* Since 1950 there has been a great influx of urban traders, state officials, administrators, politicians, social reformers and educators in Banari, which was accelerated by the opening of a modern communication system and extension of state-sponsored community development programmes in the region. These people from the urban centres created another role for the intertribal market : that of an agent of culture change in the region. As is apparent from the facts related in Chapters V, VI and VII, the new role, since 1950, of the Banari intertribal market does not originate in any ecological or cultural needs of the tribal and peasant communities of the region ; rather, it appears primarily because of the concerted programmes of directed culture change by the state. Whatever the situations in which change occurs, my concern here, for theoretical purposes, is primarily with the processes of culture change operating at the Banari intertribal market, be they pre- or post-1950.

During recent decades, considerable writings have appeared on various processes of culture change (Keesing 1953). But most of them are based on inferences rather than upon observation of the actual processes by which cultural change was made effective. In some of the earliest studies on the subject, Wissler (1923), for example, who charted the patterns of moccasins over the Plains and the adjacent culture areas, and Hallowell (1926), who studied regional variation in bear ceremonialism in North America and Asia, gave us an idea of how cultural elements were modified as they moved from one tribe to others, but they hardly revealed the mechanism of how and when this happened, and by whom the change was brought about.

An important attempt to define the problems in understanding processes of culture change was the memorandum on acculturation prepared by Redfield, Linton, and Herskovits (1936). This was more of a guide-line for future investigation rather than an exposition of the problem itself. From then on, theories and concepts on culture change have appeared in considerable diversity from Kroober's concept of "stimulus diffusion" (1940) to Eaton's concept of "controlled acculturation" (1952).

In his classic, the *Dynamics of Culture Change* (1945), Malinowski described the processes of culture contact and change in Africa. However, in the case studies reported in this study he hardly illustrated the actual process of culture contact or change. He only described the major steps in any processes of change. Others, like M. T. Hodgen (1945 : 466), who used documentary evidences in studying the processes of diffusion of paper and glass in England, advanced, at a very general level, three steps in culture change : exposure, establishment, and dissemination. Subsequently (1952 : 121), she stated that a scientific investigation of the processes of culture change or acculturation "can best be carried on among historical peoples, where the dated evidence is abundant, not among non-literate folk, where it is either scarce or absent".

More recently Homer Barnett (1953) published a theoretical treatise on "innovation" which he considers the basis and being of culture change. But, like all previous studies, his reporting on processes of change has been retrospective only, that is, dealing with completed research, usually far back in time. Although Robert Redfield (1930 : 12) pointed out several decades ago that "It would seem a more direct procedure to study such processes [of culture change] as they actually occur, rather than to content oneself with comparing the historical sequences so laboriously determined by the historical methods of the ethnologist", very few anthropologists attempted such a study. Spicer's (1952) case studies on technological change, and Paul's (1955) case materials on *Health, Culture and Community* merit mention here. However, more extensive and intensive data on the processes of culture change are needed, not only for theoretical clarification but also for their applied significance in the context of directed culture change where economic and other development depend so much on successful introduction of new ideas and practices.

III

On the basis of case studies reported in Chapters VI, VII and VIII, I have distinguished two basic processes of culture change operating at the Banari intertribal market. I shall call the first the processes of economic change, and the second the processes of social change. In the economic sphere there are certain principles which govern economic change. These arise out of transactions at the intertribal market between individuals and groups of individuals. These transactions in turn act as catalysts to change the secular and religious values of the participants, and, in turn, through them, the tribes and castes of the region. Extending this line of thought further, I may state as a second hypothesis :

> The processes of change in the economic sphere function through transactions between individuals involving the material sphere of life, on the one hand, and the system of values of the regional culture, on the other. Change restricted to the religious sphere and to certain social spheres of life, such as education and administration, operates primarily in terms of a change of values of the people of the regional culture.
>
> —Hypothesis II

The processes of change at the intertribal market are implemented by individuals or groups of individuals whom I have called change agents. They can be considered as functioning within the appropriate spheres of change as delimited for purposes of analysis, although a change agent may operate and influence one or more aspects of a culture. For example, a Phariya, an economic change agent, who operates in adjusting the native economy to the modern market economy, sometimes also changes the social values of the tribes and castes of the region. The role of change agents, as observed at the Banari intertribal market, thus suggests another hypothesis for future testing :

> The physical focus of a regional culture will reflect the nature of the independence and interdependence of its components and the processes of equilibrium and change, as well as the change agents. The role of the change agents may be singular or manifold.
>
> —Hypothesis III

Processes of Economic Change

The tribes and castes of the region have traditionally carried out economic transactions among themselves on the basis of direct or serial barters. The economic transactions at the market margins operate on this principle of barter. However, there are other sets of people, such as itinerant urban traders, who carry out economic transactions with the tribes and castes of the region at the market centre strictly on the basis of money. In this multicentric economy the change from barter to money is effected by an intricate process undertaken by the Phariya, which I have described in Chapter VII. A Phariya changes natives' commodities into cash and facilitates natives' transactions with an urban trader. By this economic process the Phariya assists in changing the economic principles of barter to money, from a multicentric to a unicentric economy. Through the same process a Phariya changes the tribes' and peasant's use of special purpose money to general purpose money and regulates price by idiosyncratic personal considerations to the concept of price in relation to supply and demand. A Phariya introduces the modern market characteristics of standardization of products ; of measurement in terms of weight rather than volume ; of the middleman ; of banking and credit ; and of advertising for mass-manufactured commodities. Although the role of a Phariya is specialized, operating specially to effect a smooth change from the native economy to the modern self-regulating economy, an urban trader, or a person who transacts on modern market principles, could operate as an economic change agent and stimulate the processes of economic change at the intertribal market.

Processes of Social Change

As detailed in Chapter VII, the processes of social change at the Banari intertribal market are operated by secular and religious change agents. A change agent, such as a community development worker, sometimes arranges demonstrations of improved fertilizers and explains their effectiveness in producing better crops to the peasant peoples of the region and thereby not only attempts to change but also changes their values towards modern techniques of cultivation and agriculture. Sometimes he organizes exhibitions on health and medicine in order to change the people's values of public health. At other times he convenes meetings with tribesmen and explains the system of public administration in order to change their secular ideas and perhaps to create familiarity and respect for the administrative system of which they are a part. Through these such special processes as demonstration, exhibition, explanation, and the like a community development worker operates to effect changes in the social values of tribes and castes of the region. Likewise, other secular change agents, such as a political leader, a congressman, or a policeman, a postal or revenue official operate at the market place to change the people's values in their respective, secular affairs. A political leader uses the cock, a sacred bird of the hill tribes, as his election symbol, prepares his manifesto in the form of a folksong and addresses the tribesmen in their native dialect in order to effect change in the political values of the tribesmen. The techniques used by secular change agents may differ, but they basically reflect similiar social processes, characterized by effective communication between them and the peoples of the region.

Unlike a secular change agent, a religious change agent operates on both direct and indirect processes of social change. When, for example, a European missionary preaches his tenets and sings sacred songs along with his converts at the intertribal market, he uses direct process to change the religious values of the tribesmen. On the other hand, when a Hindu landlord builds a temple at the market place, or a Hindu trader circulates leaflets on the Hindu view of cosmology, they, as religious change agents, use an indirect process of social change at the intertribal market and one which is largely covert in operation and effect.

In contrast to the secular change agent, the results of the processes of the social change operated by the economic change agent are virtually always indirects. When a Phariya exchanges a native's commodity for cash, he not only engages in an economic transaction but he is also translating urban values into local ones. He introduces among the tribesmen the abstract, alien concept of money as a medium, measure, standard and store. The indirect process of social change is reflected still more in the situation where an economic change agent introduces an innovation—for example, the cultivation of cash crops among the tribesmen of the region. He indirectly changes their traditional values of producing consumption commodities rather than cash commodities. One of the most interesting examples of the indirect processes of social change is revealed in the case of the Birhor whose values of conservation of wild animals changed radically when an export market for monkeys was created by an economic change agent. The Birhors in a very short period not only eliminated all the monkeys from the region, but also found that their source of livelihood can also be found outside the forests. This leads us to another hypothesis :

> The effect of change agents may be discerned in either covert or overt culture or both
>
> —Hypothesis IV

The Banari intertribal market operates in two major cultural spheres, one in the context of regional socio-economic values of componential tribes and castes, and the other in the context of modern urban values introduced by change agents. It is obvious that the urban values are strikingly different from those of the tribes and castes of the region. The operation on the first sphere is reflected in the socio-economic activities at the market margins, where each tribe and caste of the region maintains its cultural identity by following the traditional pattern of social and economic specialization, but where, at the same time, each of these tribes and castes, through traditional practices of economic independence and sharing regional traditional festivals and similar activities, blends as an interdependent regional culture. In this first sphere the analysis has shown that the Banari intertribal market helps maintain eco-cultural balance in the region.

The operation on the second sphere is evidenced by the socio-economic interactions among the urban agents and the peasant, artisan, and tribesmen of the region at the market centre, where the intertribal market stimulates culture change in the region. On the basis of this study of the Banari intertribal market, a final hypothesis is advanced :

> When an institution serves only peoples belonging to its region, it creates and maintains interdependence among them ; when an institution serves peoples of whom at least one is guided by values originating outside its region, it operates to bring about culture change or, specifically, acculturation in its region.
>
> —Hypothesis V

This fifth hypothesis, after further testing, may explain both the phenomena of stability and change which are often discussed but seldom resolved in any theory of culture dynamics (Herskovits 1948 : 18). Lange's illuminating paper on the analysis of culture dynamics (1954 : 292) has shown how cultural stability and change operate hand in hand among the Pueblo, Indians of the United States, suggesting that stability and change are not phenomena unique to the situation I have observed in Chota Nagpur.

While Lange's study supports my fifth hypothesis, the possible, general validity of any of the hypotheses I have advanced earlier should, of course, be tested by many more studies of intertribal markets in different parts of India and in other parts of the world for confirmation or modification in a specific cultural context.

Chapter X

SUMMARY AND CONCLUSION

The present study shows that the Banari intertribal market is not only a centre of redistribution of economic resources of the region which it serves; it is also a centre of social, religious, and political activity of the tribes and castes of the region. In brief, the Banari intertribal market operates as a multi-purpose institution of the region.

Traditionally, in economic parlance, the Banari intertribal market can be understood as a market place, a site where buyers and sellers meet. Barter and exchange characterize the economic transaction of commodities. However, in contemporary situations the Banari market may be viewed economically as belonging to a multicentric economy (Bohannan 1962 : 15), or dual economy (Boeke 1953 : 87 ; Furnivall 1944 : 41), where tribes and castes of the region use barter in transferring general purpose commodities among themselves, and use the "market principle" in transferring special purpose commodities from the urban traders. In other words, the Banari intertribal market has distinct multi-transactional spheres.

Socio-culturally the Banari intertribal market is understood as an institution facilitating social continuity of tribes and castes in the region, and also as an institution creating a regional culture.

During recent years, having been exposed to various urban economic, social, political, and religious values, the Banari intertribal market has served as an agent of culture change in the region. The processes of culture change operating at the market can be identified in two spheres : (1) the processes of economic change, where the traditionally operating economic principle of barter is being changed to the principles of the modern self-regulating market, (Polanyi, Arensberg and Pearson 1957) ; and (2) the processes of social change where secular and religious values of the tribes and castes of the region are being changed into modern urban and social values. A network of economic, secular, and religious change agents, operating at the intertribal market, facilitate culture change in the region. Both direct and indirect processes of change are identified at the intertribal market. These processes of economic and social, and direct and indirect, change are shown to account for the culture change operating in the intertribal market.

Finally, this study, which has been based on an intensive investigation of the Banari intertribal market, substantiates the following hypotheses formulated in the first chapter : first, an intertribal market is a centre not only of economic but also of social, religious, and political activity in the region ; second, an intertribal market helps to create and maintain networks of socio-economic ties among the peoples of the region ; and, third, an intertribal market is an institutional agent of cultural change. The study has also shown that an institution, such as the Banari intertribal market, which maintains cultural continuity, can also be instrumental in bringing about culture change or, specifically, acculturation, in its region. While it has substantiated my early hypotheses, the analysis has led to certain hypotheses which warrant further testing in the future. I have enumerated them in the previous chapter and they follow here :

> Different ethnic groups can live in a region and share a regional culture through regular or recurrent contact at a focal point of that region and yet maintain their own particular, distinctive cultures. The sharing of a regional culture, however, and its continuing equilibrium is dependent on the particular contribution each of the component ethnic groups makes to the whole. Such equilibrium is likely to be disrupted through contact from outside the region at the point of contact, that is, the focal point of the regional culture.
>
> —Hypothesis I

> The processes of change in the economic sphere function through transactions between individuals involving the material sphere of life, on the one hand, and the system of values of the regional culture, on the other. Change restricted to the religious sphere and to certain social spheres of life, such as education and administration, operates primarily in terms of a change of values of the people of the regional culture.
>
> —Hypothesis II

The physical focus of a regional culture will reflect the nature of the independence and interdependence of its components and the processes of equilibrium and change, as well as the change agents. The role of the change agents may be singular or manifold.

—Hypothesis III

The effect of change agents may be discerned in either covert or overt culture or both.

—Hypothesis IV

When an institution serves only peoples belonging to its region, it creates and maintains interdependence among them; when an institution serves peoples of whom at least one is guided by values originating outside its region, it operates to bring about culture change or, specifically, acculturation, in its region.

—Hypothesis V

GLOSSARY

Of Technical and Local Terms

Bahngi : A Bahngi is a device for carrying loads, placed or hung at the two ends of a pole, which is balanced on shoulders of any individual.

Cultural Centre : The Cultural centre of a region, as understood in this study, includes peoples technologically more advanced than those living in its cutural margins. It is also a centre of secular and religious activities in the region.

Cultural Margins : The Cultural margins of a region include peoples who are technologically more backward than those living in its cultural centre. They remain in close contact with the peoples in the cultural centre and join them in regional activities.

Ecological Centre : The Ecological centre of a region refers to that part of its geographical territory where human exploitation of nature through domestication of plants and animals is more evident than in its counterpart, ecological margins. In Banari, the valley constitutes the ecological centre of the region.

Ecological Margins : The Ecological margins of a region refers to that part of its territory where domestication of animals and plants by human populations is limited ; wild animals and plants abound ; and communication is limited. The concept of the ecological margins is relative to the ecological centre of a region.

Market Centre : The Market centre refers to the urban zone of the market place where economic transactions are carried out according to the modern market principles of supply and demand and use of money, etc. For Market principles, see, Polanyi, Arensberg and Pearson (1957). Also see, Market place.

Market, Intertribal : The Intertribal market is an institution, widely found in Chota Nagpur and its adjacent territories, which brings together peoples from different ethnic origins, for not only economic but also secular and religious activities in the region. The term is also used to refer to (1) the place or location where tribesmen and castesmen meet on a regular cycle of days to transact their socio-economic business ; (2) the principle of economic transactions where general purpose commodities are traded by barter and the special purpose commodities are traded for money.

Market Margins : The Market margins refer to the native zone, that is, Phariya, Peasant, Artisan and hill tribal or marginal zones, of the market place where economic transactions are mostly carried out according to barter and exchange of commodities. Also see, Market place.

Market Place : A Market place refers to the location where different peoples from a region, itinerant urban traders from towns and cities, and public officials from outside the region meet once or twice a week to transact socio-economic activity. There are two broad divisions of a market place, one, called the *market centre*, occupied by the peoples from outside the region ; and the other called the *market margins*, occupied by the tribes and castemen from the region.

Market, Self-Regulating : A self-regulating market is a system of human economic activity governed by the supply and demand price mechanism. Because economic activities and other aspects of life are closely interrelated, a self-regulating market tends to influence all other activities to a much greater degree than the economy would, under other types of economic systems.

Naye Paise : A denomination of the Indian coin, a hundredth part of a Rupee. Roughly five Naye Paise are equivalent to a United States' cent

Paila : The Pailas are wooden, metal, or bamboo containers of varying sizes used by the peoples of Banari which measure commodities by volume. These are the most commonly used measuring device of the tribesmen of the region.

Panchayat : A Panchayat is a council of elders, organized on the basis of a village or a group of villages, which regulates judicial and administrative problems of its peoples. There are also Panchayats organized on the basis of tribe or caste. In popular speech the former meaning is referred to.

Pargana : It is a revenue division, comprising 50 to 100 square miles, which served as an administrative unit during pre-British India.

Phariya : The word Phariya, literally translatable as mediator, designates a small group of regional people, who have developed distinctive rules and patterns of behaviour and interaction in the market situation in the region. They facilitate socio-economic communication between the tribes, artisan and peasant peoples of the region and the urban peoples who trade and visit the intertribal market. A Phariya, serving as a change agent, helps to reduce and stabilize the pressures of acculturation in the region.

Region : A region for the purpose of this inquiry is defined as the area catered by an intertribal market, both in ecological and cultural terms.

Settlements : See village types.

Tribe : A tribe in Chota Nagpur, especially in the Banari region, may be defined as an endogamous group of people, having distinctive dialect and other socio-economic characteristics. Also, a tribe shares habitat and a common language with other ethnic groups of the region and forms an interdependent socio-economic tie with them.

Village, Dispersed : A dispersed village refers to a geographical unit where homesteads are widely dispersed from one another. Its boundaries are arbitrarily defined by revenue authorities.

Village, Mixed : A mixed village refers to a human settlement whose populations belong to different ethnic and religious groups, e.g., a village including two or more tribes or caste groups.

Village, Nucleated : A nucleated village refers to a human settlement where homesteads belonging to the persons living therein are clustered at a particular place.

Zamindar : A Zamindar means a landlord who, under the pre-independence administrative system of the Indian States, had the right to impose and collect revenues on any natural resources utilized by the residents of his territory. He formerly played, and in many ways continues to play, a vital role in the economic, political, and also social life of the region.

BIBLIOGRAPHY

BARNETT, H. G., 1953, *Innovation: the basis of Cultural Change*, New York, McGraw Hill Inc., 462 pp

BAUER, P. T., 1954, *West African Trade*. Cambridge, Cambridge University Press, 450 pp.

BENEDICT, RUTH, 1934, *Patterns of Culture*. New York, Houghton Mifflin, 290 pp.

BIRT, FRANCIS BRADLEY, 1903, *Chota Nagpore: A Little Known Province of the Empire*. London, Smith, Elder, 487 pp.

BOAS, FRANZ, 1898, *The North-western Tribes of Canada, Twelfth and Final Report*. London, British Association of the Advancement of Sciences, Proceedings I : 40-61.

BOEKE, J. H., 1953, *Economics and Economic Policy in Dual Societies*. New York, Institute of Pacific Relations, 324 pp.

BOHANNAN, PAUL, 1959, *The Impact of Money on an African Subsistence Economy. The Journal of Economic History* 19 : 498-503.

BOHANNAN, PAUL AND GEORGE DALTON, Eds., 1962, *Markets in Africa* Evanston, North-western University Press, 762 pp.

DALTON, E. T., 1872, *Descriptive Ethnology of Bengal*. Calcutta, Office of the Superintendent of Government Printing, 327 pp.

DEWEY, ALICE G., 1962, *Peasant Marketing in Java*. New York, The Free Press of Glencoe, Inc., 238 pp

DRIVER, W. H. P., 1888, *Birhor. Journal of the Royal Asiatic Society of Bengal* 47, 1 : 12-38.

EATON, J. W., 1952, *Controlled Acculturation : A Survival Technique of the Hutterites. American Sociological Review* 17 : 331-40.

EINZIG, PAUL, 1949, *Primitive Money in its Ethnological, Historical and Economic Aspects*. London, Eyre & Spottsworde, 517 pp.

Encyclopedia of the Social Sciences, Vol. 10, 1933, New York, McMillan Company.

FIRTH, RAYMOND, 1939, *Primitive Polynesian Economy*. New York, Humanities Press, 387 pp.

————1946, *Malay Fishermen: Their Present Economy*. London, Kegan, Paul, Trench, Trubner and Co., Ltd., 354 pp.

FOGG, WALTER, 1941, *Changes in the Layout, Characteristics and Functions of a Moroccan Tribal Market, Consequent on European Control, Man* 41 : 104-108.

FOSTER, G. M., 1948, *The Folk Economy of Rural Mexico, with Special Reference to Marketing. Journal of Marketing* 13 : 153-162.

FURNIVALL, J. S., 1944, *Netherlands India, A Study of Plural Economy*. New York, The Macmillan Company, 502 pp.

GLUCKMAN, MAX, 1958, *Analysis of a Social Situation in Modern Zululand. Rhodes-Livingstone Paper No. 28*. Manchester, Manchester University Press, 72 pp.

GOODFELLOW, D. M., 1939, *Principles of Economic Sociology.* Philadelphia, P. Blakistan, 289 pp.

HALLOWELL, A. I., 1926, *Bear Ceremonialism in the Ncrthern Hemisphere. American Anthropologist* 28 : 1-175

HERSKOVITS, MELHILLE J., 1941, *Economics and Anthropology : A Rejoinder- Journal of Political Economy* 49 : 269-78.

———1952, *Economic Anthropology.* New York, Alfred A. Knopf, 547 pp.

———1955, *Cultural Anthropology.* New York, Alfred A. Knopf, 569 pp.

HODGEN, M. T., 1945, *Glass and Paper : An Historical Study of Acculturation, South-western Journal of Anthropology* 1 : 466-97.

———1952, *Change and History.* Viking Fund Publication in Anthropology No. 18. New York, Wenner-Gren Foundation of Anthropological Research, 324 pp.

HOGEIN, H. I., 1958, *Social Change.* London, Watts and Company, 257 pp.

HONIGMANN, J., 1959, *The World of Man.* New York, Harper and Row, 971 pp.

KEESING, FELIX M., 1953, *Culture Change : An Analysis and Bibliography of Anthropological Sources.* Stanford, Stanford University Press, 242 pp.

KLUCKHOHN, RICHARD, 1962, *The Konso Economy of Southern Ethiopia. African Markets,* Paul Bohannan and George Dalton, eds. Evanston, North-western Universiy Press : 409-28.

KNIGHT, FRANK, 1941, *Anthropology and Economics. Journal of Political Economy* 49 : 247-68.

KROEBER, A. L., 1940, *Stimulus diffusion. American Anthropologist* 42 ; 116-21.

LANGE, CHARLES H., 1954, *The Analysis and Application of Cultural Dynamics. The Texus Journal of Science* 6 : 3 : 292-96.

LEUVA, K. K., 1962, *The Asurs.* New Delhi, Adim Jati Sevak Sangh, 234 pp.

MAJUMDAR, D. N., 1937, *A Tribe in Transition.* Calcutta, Orient Longmans, 216 pp.

———1950, *The Affairs of a Tribe.* Lucknow, Universal Publishers, 367 pp.

MALINOWSKI, BRONISLAW, 1926, *The Primitive Economics of the Trobriand Islanders. Economic Journal* 31 : 1-16.

———1945, *The Dynamics of Culture Change.* New Haven, Yale University Press, 171 pp.

MEAD, MARGARET, 1930, *Melanesian Middlemen.* Natural History 30 : 115-30.

———1937, *Co-operation and Competition Among Primitive Peoples.* New York, McGraw-Hill Book Company, Inc., 531 pp.

———1956, *New Lives for Old.* New York, William Morrow and Company, 548 pp.

MIKESELL, MARVIN W., 1958, *The Role of Tribal Markets in Mexico—Examples from Northern zone. Geographical Review* 28 : 494-511.

MINTZ, S. W., 1957, *The Role of the Middleman in the Internal Distribution System of a Caribbean Peasant Economy. Human Organization* 15 : 2 : 18-23.

MINTZ, S., 1959, *Internal Market Systems as Mechanisms of Social Articulation. Intermediate Societies, Social Mobility and Communication*, V. F. Ray, ed. Seattle, American Ethnological Society, Proceedings : 20-30.

OTTENBERG, SIMON and PHOEBE, 1962, *Afikpo Markets : 1900-60. African Markets*, Paul Bohannan and George Dalton, eds. Evanston, Northwestern University Press : 110-69.

PAUL, B. J. (Ed.), 1955, *Health, Culture and Community*. New York, Russell Sage Foundation, 493 pp.

POLANYI, KARL, 1957, *The Great Transformation*. Boston, Beacon Press, 315 pp.

POLANYI, KARL ; ARENSBERG, CONRAD M., and PEARSON, HARRY W. (Eds.), 1957, *Trade and Market in the Early Empires*. Glencoe, The Free Press, 382 pp.

REDFIELD, ROBERT, 1930, *Tepotzlan, a Mexican Village*, Chicago, Chicago University Press, 247 pp.

——— 1960, *The Little Community and Peasant Society and Culture*. Chicago, Chicago University Press : 77 and 188 pp. (paperback).

REDFIELD, ROBERT, LINTON, R. and HERSKOVITS, M. J., 1936, *A Memorandum on Acculturation. American Anthropologist* 38 : 149-52.

REID, J., 1908, *Final Report on the Survey and Settlement Operations in the District of Ranchi* (1902-10). Calcutta, Government Printing Press, 187 pp.

RENNEL, 1781, *Map of Hindustan*. Located at the National Library of India, Calcutta.

RICHARDS, A. I. (Ed.), 1953, *Economic Development and Change*. Cambridge, Cambridge University Press, 301 pp.

RISLEY, HERBERT, 1911, *The People of India*. London, W. Thacker, 472 pp.

ROY, S. C., 1912, *The Mundas and Their Country*. Calcutta, City Book Society, 546 pp.

——— 1915, *The Oraons of Chota Nagpur*. Ranchi, published by the author, 491 pp.

——— 1925, *The Birhors : A Little Known Jungle Tribe of Chota Nagpur*, Ranchi, Man in India, 608 pp.

——— 1928, *Oraon Religion and Customs*. Ranchi, Man in India, 418 pp.

——— 1937, *The Kharias* (2 volumes), Ranchi, Man in India, 687 pp.

SIEGEL, B. J., 1955, *Acculturation : Critical Abstracts*. Stanford, Stanford University Press, 231 pp.

SINGH, R. P. 1958, *Structure, Drainage and Morphology of the Chota Nagpur Highlands. Geographical Outlook* 2 : 3 : 23-32.

SINHA, D. P., 1958, *Cultural Ecology of the Birhor : A Methodological Illustration. Journal of Social Research* 1 : 1 : 86-96.

——— 1959, *Research and Development in Anthropology : A Case of Birhor Resettlement. Journal of Social Research* 2 : 1 : 98-103.

———1961, *Unity and Extension of a Tribal Village in Chota Nagpur*, Manuscript, 18 pp.

——— 1963, *The Role of Phariya in Tribal Acculturation in a Central Indian Market. Ethnology* 2 : 2 : 178-79.

SINHA, S., DASGUPTA, B. K., and BANNERJEE, H. N., 1961, *Agriculture, Crafts and Weekly Market of South Manbhum, Bulletin of the Anthropological Survey of India* 10 : 1 : 1-163.

SPICER, E. H. (Ed.), 1952, *Human Problems in Technological Change.* New York, Russell Sage Foundation, 301 pp.

STEINER, FRANZ, 1954, *Notes on Comparative Economics. British Journal of Sociology* 5 : 118-29.

TANDON, J. S., 1960, *Ceremonial Friendship among the Bhattra of Bastar, Journal of Social Research* 3 : 1 : 38-54.

TAX, SOL, 1953, *Penny Capitalism : A Guatemalan Indian Economy.* Washington, Smithsonian Institution. Institute of Social Anthropology Publication No. 16, 230 pp.

THOMPSON, LAURA, 1961, *Towards a Science of Mankind*, New York McGraw-Hill Book Co., 276 pp.

THURNWALD, RICHARD, 1932, *Economics in Primitive Communities.* London, Oxford University Press, 314 pp.

VIDYARTHI, L. P., 1958, *Cultural Types in Tribal Bihar. Journal of Social Research* 1 : 75-85.

VOGET, F., 1950, *A Shoshone Innovator. American Anthropologist* 52 : 1 : 53-63.

WATSON, WILLIAM, 1958, *Tribal Cohesion in a Money Economy.* Manchester, Manchester University Press, 246 pp.

WILSON, GODFREY, and MONICA, 1945, *An Analysis of Social Change.* Cambridge, Cambridge University Press, 177 pp.

WISSLER, CLARK, 1923, *Man and Culture.* New York, Thomas Y. Crowell, 493 pp.

ZAHAR, D., 1954, *Notes sur les Marches Mossi du Yaterga. Africa* 24 : 4 : 370-76.

INDEX

ACCULTURATION, 58, 93, 95 103
Adar, 45, 87
Administration, 73
Advertising, 53, 67, 97
Agriculturists, 38, 59
Agricultural commodities, 44
Agricultural produce, 50
Arensberg, Conrad, 6, 13, 101, 111
Artisans, 35, 44, 58
Astrology, 78, 99
Asur, 24, 31, 33, 38, 52, 53, 54, 60, 61, 66
Audience, 76
Australian National University, xi

BAHNGI, 49, 105
Banari, 34, 40; ethnic components, 29, landlord, 53; market, viii, 1, 13, 41, 44; market history 37; region, 29
Bania, 35; also see trader
Bank, 65, 67, 97
Bannerjee, H. N., 112
Bard, 77
Barnett, H., 95, 109
Barter, 38, 59, 60, 62, 81, 89, 97, 101; serial, 63, 97
Bauer, P. T., 109
Benedict, Ruth., 10, 109
Benti, 90
Birjia, 31, 33, 37, 49, 53, 71
Birhor, 14, 24, 31, 33, 38, 52, 54, 60, 63, 71, 81
Birt, F. B., 109
Block Development Officer, 41
Boas, Franz., 10, 109
Boeke, J. H., 109
Bohannan, Paul., 10, 12, 38, 109
Bride price, 86
British Raj, 41
Birth, 85, 88

CASH, 62
Cash crop, 25, 26
Cattle, 27
Ceremonial friendship, 71, 90
Change agents, 64, 69, 73, 75, 96, 99, 103; also see economic change agent; extension agent; religious change agent; secular change agent; social change agent
Chik-Baraik, 32, 35, 38, 47, 60, 89
Christianity, 78
Chota Nagpur, 31, 47, 92; area 7; map 8
Climate, 20, 21
Collective hunt, 83
Commodities, 55, 61 ; Surplus 67 ; also see general purpose commodity; special purpose commodity
Communication, 58, 72
Communications, mass, 39
Communities, 29, 33
Community Development, 35, 43, 53, 56, 65; agent, 56, 80
Comparative economics,
Competition, 59
Conflicts and disputes, 39
Congress, 75
Contract, 45
Contractor, 41, 47, 49, 56
Crawford, J. G., xii
Credit, 67, 84, 91
Crops, cash, 25; primary, 23, 26; secondary, 58
Cultural centre, 30, 33, 34, 36; defined, 105
Cultural components, 92
Cultural continuity, 102
Cultural margins, 30, 33, 34; defined 105
Cultural region, 36
Cultural spheres, 99
Cultural values, 61, 102

8

Cultural variation, 93
Culture change, 75, 93, 95, 102; processes of, 96
Culture contact, 95
Culture: covert or overt, 99, 103

Dalton, E. T., 15, 32, 81, 109
Dalton, George, 12, 109
Dark, P. J. C., xi
Dasgupta, B. K., 112
Death, 87, 88
Demand and supply, 59, 82; also see supply and demand
Dewey, A., 12, 109
Dialects, 16, 30; Austric, 32; Asuri, 30; Birhori, 30; Kurukh, 16; Mundari, 30; Sadani, 16
Diffusion, 95
Dispute, 88
Dress, 30
Driver, W. H., 81, 107
Directed change, 57, 91
Dual economy, 101

Eaton, J. W., 95, 109
Ecological centre, 17, 21, 93; characteristics, 27; described, 25; defined, 105
Ecological components, 92
Ecological margins, 93; characteristics, 27; defined, 105; described, 23
Ecological setting, 17
Ecological variation, 93
Economic anthropology, 1, 10
Economic balance, 59
Economic change, 68; processes of, 96, 97, 101
Economic change agent, 44, 64, 66, 73, 79, 84, 96, 98, 101
Economic development, vii, 11
Economic interdependence, 63, 68
Economic role, 79
Economic stability, 59
Economic theory, 12
Economy; dual, 101; market, 63; market less, 13; multicentric, 97, 101; native, 63, 68; regional 64; subsistence, 80; unicentric, 91
Einzig, P., 109
Election, 57, 76
Elevation, 20
Elopement, 86
Employment exchange, 68
Endogamy, 70
Ethnology, regional, 3, 58
Exchange, medium of 38
Export commodity, 25
Extension agent, 75

Family, 84
Festivals, 38, 57, 58, 72
Firth, Raymond, 12
Fishing economy, Malayan, 12
Fogg, W., 109
Folklore, 32, 35, 37, 109
Folk culture, 33
Folk sellers, 49
Food gatherers, 59, also see Birhor
Footpath, 37
Forest produce, 83
Forest range, 35, 49, 56
Foster, G. H., 109
Fulbright, xi
Furnivall, J. S., 101, 109

Gandhi, Mahatma, 75
Garo, 19
General purpose commodity, 60, 62, 101
General purpose money, 38
Ghaghra, 19
Gift, 71
Glossary, 105
Gluckman, M., 109
Goats, 27
Good fellow, D. M., 12, 110.
Government, 35, 80; agents, 39; welfare, 83
Gunther, Hans., xii

Hallowell, I., 94, 110
Health education, 77

Herskovits, M. J., 11, 93, 95, 100, 110
Hindu, 35, 41, 47; castes, 32; Rajput, 34, 35, 36; population, 33
Hills and plateaus, 31, 44
Hinterland, 17, 20, 38, 44; defined, 17; map, 18; ecological pattern, 28; population, 25
Hodgen, M. T., 95, 110
Hogbin, H. I., 110
Honigmann, J., 93, 110
Horticulture, 31
Hypothesis, 13, 93, 96, 97, 99, 100, 102, 103

Industrialization, vii
Innovation, 66, 95
Intertribal market, delned, 105; absence of, 30; and forest, 24; hypothesis, 13; institution, vii, xi, 32, 38, 100, 102; seasonal variation, 56
Iron smelting, 23
Itinerant traders, 39, 64, 97; also see urban traders
Interdependence, 32, 93
Interview, 15

Jharkhand, 75
Jehangutua, 90

Keesing, F. M., 94, 110
Kharia, 31, 33
Kheja, 55
Kinsmen, 39
Kisan, 49, 88
Kluckhohn, R., 110
Knight, F., 108
Kol, 82
Kroeber, A. L., 95, 102, 110
Kumba, 81
Kumhar, 35; also see Potter

Lange, C. H., xi, 100, 102, 110
Landlord, 53, 56, 77, 99
Leuva, K. K., 110
Life cycle, 85
Life history, 88
Lingua Franca, 30
Linguistic groups, 30; Austro-asiatic Munda, 30; Dravidian Oraon, 30; Indo-European Sadani, 30
Little community, 33, 34
Lohardaga, 19, 37, 40, 45, 67
Lohra, 35, 52, 54, 61, 63
Land, cultivable, Don, 26 ; Tanr, 26

Mahli, 24, 32, 34, 47, 49, 54, 60, 62, 70, 72, 84, 89
Mail, 74
Maize, 23
Majumdar, D. N., 7, 110
Malinowski, B., 10, 11, 95, 110
Market, 9; capital, 11; centre, 105; also see Market centre; economic role, 59; economy, 11, 97; institution, 9, 11, 58; intertribal, 105; also see intertribal market; margins, 105; also see market margins; peak, 52; peasant, 12, 92; also see peasant market; place, 106; also see market margins; principle, 63, 91, 101; recreation, 72; rhythm, 58; seasons, 15, 56; self regulating, 13; also see self regulating market; system, 35; tributary, 15 zones, 43, 56
Market centre, 43, 46, 50, 51, 53, 56, 97; defined, 105
Market margins, 44, 47, 50, 51, 55; defined, 105
Market place, 13, 40-44, 56, 101; defined, 105; map, 42
Marriage, 69, 86, 88, 90
Mass manufacture, 83
Material culture, 84
Mead, M., 10, 11, 110
Methods, 14
Middleman, 65, 87
Migration, 82
Mintz, S., 110

Missionary, 73, 78
Money : 38, 59, 64, 79 ; general purpose, 97 ; special purpose, 97
Money lender, 53, 67
Monkeys, 81
Monopoly, 67
Monsoon, 37, 58, 83
Morwai, 19
Multicentric economy, 97, 101
Munda, 31, 53, 89

NATIVE, 40, 41, 58
Native economy, 59, 97
Native wares, 52
Naye Paise, 105
Nehru, 47, 95
Neterhat, 45
News, 79
Newspaper, 36
Nomadism, 81, 87
North Koel River, 19, 20, 23, 25, 32, 37

OBSERVATION, 34
Occupation, 35
Occupational bases, 31
Oraon, 32, 34, 37, 46, 49, 51, 53, 70, 72, 78, 89
Oliver, Douglas,
Ottenberg, S. and P., 111

PACHAURA, 70 ; see tribal council
Paila, 50, 55, 60, 62, 84 ; described, 106
Panchayat, 53, 106
Pargana, 106
Patrilineage, 81
Paul, B. J., 95, 111
Pearson, H. W., 13, 101, 111
Peasant communities, 94 ; culture, 33, 36 ; economy, 12, 58 ; village, 36
Phariya, 2, 44, 46, 50, 54, 59, 66, 68, 73, 79, 96, 99 ; defined, 106 ; functions, 64
Pigs, 27
Polanyi, Karl, vii, 5, 13, 101, 111
Population, 29, 31
Post man, 53, 56
Post office, 35
Potters, see also Kumhar, 47, 54, 84, 89
Poultry, 27, 85
Price, 40, 97 ; mechanism, 59
Priest, 77
Primitive culture, 23
Primitive economics, 10, 11
Primitive economy, 12
Processes of social change ; direct and indirect, 98, 102
Production, 59
Public opinion, 76
Publicity, 76
Purchases, 55

RAINFALL, 21
Ranchi, 37, 40, 45, 47
Redfield, R., 33, 34, 94, 95, 111
Region, 17, 106
Regional centre, 36
Regional culture, 31, 93, 94, 97, 101
Reid, J., 111
Religious change agent, 73, 77, 80, 98, 101
Rennel, 111
Resettlement, 90, 91
Revenue peon, 53
Richards, A. I., 111
Risley, H., 21, 111
River, see North Koel
Roads, 37
Roy, S. C., 7, 31, 32, 38, 66, 82, 83, 111

SALE, 81
Sarju, 19
Sarna, 35
Scarcity, artificial, 66
School, 35, 76
Seasons, 21
Seasonal variation, 83
Secular change agent, 73, 75, 80, 98, 99, 101
Self-regulating market economy, 59, 63, 67 ; defined, 106

Shifting cultivation, 23
Siegel, B. J., 111
Singh, R. P., 23, 109
Sinha, D. P., viii, 2, 35, 66, 84, 90, 111
Sinha, Purnima, xii
Sinha, S., 112
Social change, 69, 73, 80; agent, 73; processes, 96, 101
Social continuity, 69
Social participation, 71
Social role, 69, 73
Social ties, 71
Social values, 97, 99, 101; also see cultural values
Sorcerer, 89
Southern Illinois University, xi
Special purpose commodity, 60, 62, 63, 101
Special purpose money, 38
Specialization, 32, 35
Spicer, E. H., 95, 112
Srivastava, B. K., xii
Standardization, 65, 97
Steiner, F., 112
Stimulus diffusion, 95
Subsistence economy, 81
Supply and demand, 55, 63, 65. 83, 95, 67; also see demand and supply
Surplus, 65, 67, 68

Tana Bhagat, 70, 78
Tanda, 81, 85, 87, 90
Tandon, J. S., 71, 90, 112
Tax, Sol., 11, 12, 112
Taxation, 74
Technology, 82
Temperature, 22
Temple, 36, 77
Tendar, 19, 87
Thompson, L., x, 93, 112
Thornwald, R., 10, 11, 112
Toll, 41
Trade, 82
Traditional market, 37
Tribal council, 70
Tribal groups, 7, 77, 27, 58, 90
Tribe, 106; horticultural, 32; agricultural, 32; semi-nomadic, 81
Trobriand islanders, 10
Turi, 32, 34, 47, 55, 60, 72, 84

Unicentric Economy, 97
Urban centre, 61, 66
Urban commodities, 44, 46
Urban traders, 44, 46, 49, 53, 56, 58, 60, 63, 66, 73, 79, 84, 90, 97

Valley, 31, 58
Values, relative, 62, 84
Vegetables, 27
Vidyarthi, L. P., 88, 112
Village, 29; defined, 106; dispersed, 29; mixed, 33, 36; nucleated, 29, 31, 33
Village deity, 35
Voget, F., 112

Watson, W., 112
Weights and measures, 59, 97
Welfare project, 39
Wilson, G., 112
Wissler, C., 94, 112
Wolfe, Alvin W., xii

Zahar, D., 112
Zamindar, 41, 107